JANEWAY

SO-BTB-419

A token for children

6-18-88			

BR
1714
.J33

Missouri Western College Library
St. Joseph, Missouri

772786

A Garland Series

Classics of Children's Literature 1621-1932

A collection of 117 titles
reprinted in photo-facsimile
in 73 volumes

Selected and arranged by
Alison Lurie
and
Justin G. Schiller

A Token for Children
by
James Janeway

with a preface for the Garland edition by
Robert Miner

The Holy Bible in Verse
by
Benjamin Harris
&

The History of The Holy Jesus
&

The School of Good Manners
by
Eleazar Moody
&

The Prodigal Daughter

with a preface for the Garland edition by
Elizabeth Williams

Garland Publishing, Inc.

New York & London
1977

772786

Missouri Western State College
ST. JOSEPH, MISSOURI 64507

Library of Congress Cataloging in Publication Data

Janeway, James, 1636?-1674.
  A token for children.

  (Classics of children's literature, 1621-1932)
  Reprint of 5 works published 1676-1771.
  Includes bibliographies.
    1. Children--Biography. 2. Children--Religious life
3. Children--Conduct of life. 4. Jesus Christ--
Poetry. 5. Theology, Puritan. I. Title. II. Series.
BR1714.J3 1977   248'.82   75-32134
ISBN 0-8240-2251-3

Printed in the United States of America

A Token for Children

Bibliographical Note:

This facsimile has been made
from a copy in
The Bodleian Library

(80.R.97.Th)

Preface

Suffer little children to come unto me.

If the Lord had anticipated James Janeway's misinterpretation of these immortal words, Christian doctrine on children might have been more scrupulously articulated. As it was, James Janeway and his seventeenth-century Puritan confreres were able to persuade themselves that these words were uttered *at* children rather than *about* them. And as a result, generations of Puritan children came to believe that the gnashing of teeth was the true music of the spheres.

"What ever you think of them, Christ doth not slight them; they are not too little to die, they are not too little to go to Hell. . . ." Thus does Janeway in the first (1671-1672) edition of *A Token for Children* admonish all "teachers of children" to "consider what a precious Jewel is committed to your charge." The cutting and

v

PREFACE

polishing of these jewels is Janeway's goal in this book which, as the full title indicates, contains case histories of children whose inspiring preoccupation with the next world blessed with joy their premature exit from this one. Other children, says Janeway, should be "put . . . upon imitating these sweet Children; let them read this book over an hundred times, and observe how they are affected."

Lest they should somehow err in their reaction, child readers of *A Token for Children* are addressed, too, in a special preface. They are exhorted not to lie, swear, keep naughty company, or break the sabbath—these, presumably, the full range of sins for which children are "not too little to go to Hell." Janeway next offers constructive suggestions: "Get by thyself, into the Chamber or Garret, and fall upon thy knees, and weep and mourn, and tell Christ thou art afraid that he doth not love thee. . . . Resolve to continue in well-doing all your dayes; then you shall be one of those sweet little ones that Christ will take into his Arms and bless and give a Kingdom, Crown and Glory too."

Thirteen upstanding children die gloriously in the 159 pages of Janeway's book. But their cries of anguish—"O, for assurance," cries fourteen-year-old Sarah Howley, who "brake a vein in her Lungs . . . and oft did spit blood" as she begged for deliverance— somehow eclipse their terminal spasms of joy. Sarah Howley's conversion to "divine rapture" and then to the brink of death takes four short pages. It takes her ten agonized pages more to teeter over the edge. But Sarah's tale is authentic, claims Janeway, as indeed are all thirteen. He cites unimpeachable sources for them, and in his preface to the second volume he scolds skeptics, suggesting that it better becomes the truly pious to keep their damnable doubts to themselves.

Each of the histories is plausibly different from the others. They range in kind from the child "whose mother had dedicated him to the Lord in her womb" and who apparently came into the world mouthing pieties, to a veteran nine-year-old "Monster of wickedness," who was "a thousand times more miserable and vile by his Sin," even, "than by his poverty." But the end results all seem to be the same: increasing piety followed by illness, lingering death, fear of damnation, eventual assurance of salvation, and a final joyful absorption directly into the bosom of Jesus.

Child readers might be forgiven for concluding from all this that piety and premature death were somehow connected, or that *carpe diem* might make as much sense as *mea culpa* under the circumstances, but whatever their conclusions, they seem to have taken at least one of Janeway's directions to heart: early editions of the book are extremely rare, presumably because they were read to pieces those hundred times each by increasingly intense little children.

Although ultimately his most enduring contribution, this collection of uplifting juvenile obituaries was not Janeway's only achievement. He appears to have been a popular nonconformist preacher following his graduation at twenty-three from Christ Church, Oxford, in 1659. He first preached during the plague year in London in 1665 and got his own meeting house in Jamaica Row, Rotherhithe, after the indulgence of

PREFACE

1672. That house was wrecked when the indulgence was withdrawn, and Janeway narrowly missed being arrested. "There was a tinge of religious melancholy in his character," reports the *Dictionary of National Biography*, "and like others of his family he became consumptive." He died in 1674, leaving no children of his own, it appears, to profit by his already famous book.

Although the product of undeniable religious melancholy, *A Token for Children* must have seemed sheer felicity to Puritan parents searching for a Spock of the spirit on which to wean their fallen children. While we have no reports of his effects on them from the mouths of babes themselves, and while scholars continue to argue his influence, Janeway himself would have died fulfilled had his child readers become, like Sarah Howley, "eminent in her diligence, teachableness, meekness and modesty," or, like an unnamed "Notorious Wicked Child," miraculously converted to "patience, Humility and Self-abhorrency. . . ."

Robert G. Miner, Jr.

PREFACE

ROBERT G. MINER, JR., has taught children's literature at the University of Connecticut and has been a syndicated children's book reviewer. Until recently he worked in the Book Department of Newsweek. He now lives in rural Connecticut where he is working on a book on Aesop's Fables and a novel about motherhood.

JAMES JANEWAY (1636?-1674)

Bibliography of His Books for Children:

A Token for Children; being an exact account of the conversion, holy and exemplary lives, and joyful deaths of several young children. London: Dorman Newman, 1672. Pp. 72. First edition.

A Token for Children. The Second Part. Being a further account . . . of several other young children, not published in the first part. London: D. Newman, 1672. Pp. 87. First edition.

PREFACE

A Token for Children. Being an Exact Account of the Conversion, Holy and Exemplary Lives and Joyful Deaths of Several Young Children. . . . To Which is Added, A Token for the Children of New England . . . Preserved and Published for the Encouragement of Piety in Other Children. Boston: Nicholas Boone, 1700. First American edition, including both parts of Janeway's original version along with the supplementary third part written by the Rev. Cotton Mather.

Selected References:

Halsey, Rosalie V. *Forgotten Books of the American Nursery.* Boston 1911.

Darton, F. J. Harvey. *Children's Books in England.* Cambridge, England, 1932.

Sloane, William. *Children's Books in England and America in the 17th Century.* New York 1955.

PREFACE

Thwaite, Mary F. *From Primer to Pleasure.* London 1965.

St. John, Judith. *The Osborne Collection of Early Children's Books 1476-1910. A Catalogue, volume II.* Toronto 1975.

These *Three* Books of the same Author Mr. *James Janeway*, are Printed for, and Sold by *Dorman Newman*.

H Eaven upon Earth, or the best friend in the worst of times; The third Edition enlarged, Price 2 *s.* 6 *d.*

Death unstung, a Sermon Preacht at the Funeral of *Thomas Mousley* an *Apothecary* : With a brief Narrative of his Life and Death : also the manner of Gods dealings with Him , before and after his Conversion : Drawn up by his own hand ; Price 1 *s.*

A Sermon Preached at the Funeral of *Thomas Savage*, Price 4 *d.*

A

TOKEN

FOR

CHILDREN:

BEING

An Exact Account of the Conver-
sion, Holy and Exemplary Lives,
and Joyful Deaths, of several
young Children.

By *James Janeway*, Minister of the
Gospel.

────── *Suffer little Children to come
unto me, and forbid them not:
for of such is the Kingdom of
God*: Mark 10.14.

LONDON,

Printed for *Dorman Newman*, at the
Kings Arms at the Corner of
Grocers Alley in the *Poul-
trey*, 1676.

To all Parents, School-masters and School-Mistresses, or any that have any hand in the Education of Children.

Dear Friends,

I Have oft thought that *Christ* speaks to you, as *Pharaoh's* Daughter did to *Moses's* Mother; Take this Child and Nurse it for me. O Sirs, consider what a precious Jewel is committed to your charge, what an advantage you have to shew your love to *Christ*, to stock the next Generation with Noble Plants, and what a joyful account you may make, if you be faithful: Remember, Souls, Christ, and Grace, cannot be over-valued. I confess you have some disadvantages, but let that only excite your

A 3   dili-

diligence ; the Salvation of Souls, the commendation of your Master, the greatneſs of your reward, and everlaſting glory, will pay for all. Remember the Devil is at work hard, wicked ones are induſtrious, and a corrupt nature is a rugged knotty piece to hew ; but be not diſcouraged, I am almoſt as much afraid of your lazineſs and unfaithfulneſs, as any thing. Do but fall to work luſtily, and who knows but that rough ſtone may prove a Pillar in the Temple of God ? In the Name of the living God, as you will anſwer it ſhortly at his Bar, I command you to be faithful in Inſtructing and Catechizing your young ones ; If you think I am too peremptory, I pray read the command from my Maſter himſelf, *Deut.* **6. 7.** Is not the duty clear ? and dare you neglect ſo direct a Command ? Are the Souls of your Children of no value ? Are you willing

that

that they fhould be Brands of Hell?
Are you indifferent whether they
be Damned or Saved? fhall the
Devil run away with them without
controul? Will not you ufe your
utmoft endeavour to deliver them
from the wrath to come? you fee
that they are not Subjects uncapa-
ble of the Grace of God; what-
ever you think of them, Chrift
doth not flight them; they are not
too little to dye, they are not too
little to go to Hell, they are not
too little to ferve their great Ma-
fter, too little to go to Heaven;
For of fuch is the Kingdom of God:
And will not a poffibility of their
Converfion and Salvation, put you
upon the greateft diligence to teach
them? Or are Chrift, and Heaven,
and Salvation, fmall things with
you? If they be, then indeed I
have done with you: but if they be
not, I befeech you lay about you
with all your might; the Devil

knows

knows your time is going apace, it will shortly be too late. O therefore what you do, do quickly ; and do it, I say, with all your *might*; O pray, pray, pray, and live holily before them , and take some time daily to speak a little to your Children, one by one , about their miserable condition by Nature: I knew a Child that was converted by this sentence, from a godly School-mistress in the Country, *Every Mothers Child of you are by Nature Children of wrath.* Put your Children upon Learning their Catechism, and the Scriptures, and getting to pray and *weep* by themselves after *Christ* : take heed of their company ; take heed of pardoning a lye ; take heed of letting them mispend the Sabbath; put them, I beseech you, upon imitating these sweet Children ; let them Read this Book over an hundred times, and observe

how

how they are *affected*, and ask them what they think of thofe Children, and whether they would not be fuch? and follow what you do with earneft cries to God, and be in travel to fee Chrift formed in their Souls. I have prayed for you, I have oft prayed for your Children, and I love them dearly; and I have prayed over thefe papers, that God would ftrike in with them, and make them effectual to the good of their Souls. Incourage your Children to read this Book, and lead them to improve it. What is prefented, is faithfully taken from experienced folid Chriftians, fome of them no way related to the Children, who themfelves were Eye and Ear-witneffes of God's works of Wonder; or from my own knowledg, or from Reverend godly Minifters, and from Perfons that are of unfpotted reputation for Holinefs, Integrity and Wifdom,

dom; and several passages are taken *verbatim* in writing from their dying Lips. I may add many other excellent Examples, if I have any encouragement in this Piece. That the young generation may be far more excellent than this, is the Prayer of one that dearly loves little Children.

James Janeway.

A

PREFACE:

Containing

DIRECTIONS

TO

CHILDREN.

YOU may now hear (my dear Lambs) what other good Children have done, and remember how they wept and prayed by themselves ; how earnestly they cryed out for an interest in the Lord Jesus Christ : May you not read how dutiful they were to their Parents ? How diligent at their Books ?

Books? how ready to learn the Scripture, and their Catechisms? Can you forget what Questions they were wont to ask? How much they feared a lye, how much they abhorred naughty company, how holy they lived, how dearly they were loved, how joyfully they died?

But tell me, my dear Children, and tell me truly, Do you do as these Children did? Did you ever see your miserable state by Nature? Did you ever get by your self and weep for sin, and pray for grace and pardon? Did you ever go to your Father and Mother, or Master, or Mistress, and beg of them to pity you, and pray for you, and to teach you what you shall do to be saved, what you shall do to get Christ, Heaven and Glory? Dost thou love to be taught good things? Come tell me truly, my dear Child; for I would fain do what I can possibly to keep thee from falling into everlasting Fire. I would fain have you one of those little ones, which Christ will

take

take into his Arms and bless: How
dost thou spend thy time? is it in play
and Idleness, and with wicked Chil-
dren? Dare you take Gods Name in
vain, or swear, or tell a lie? Dare
you do any thing which your Parents
forbid you, and neglect to do what they
command you? Do you dare to run up
and down upon the Lords day? or do
you keep in to read your book, and to
learn what your good Parents com-
mand you? What do you say, Child?
Which of these two sorts are you of?
Let me talk a little with you, and ask
you a few Questions.

1. Were not these Children sweet
Children, which feared God, and were
dutiful to their Parents? Did not their
Fathers and Mothers, and every body
that fears God, love them, and praise
them? What do you think is become
of them, now they are dead and gone?
Why, they are gone to Heaven, and
are singing Hallelujahs with the An-
gels: They see glorious things, and
having nothing but joy and pleasure,
they

they shall never sin no more, they shall never be beat any more, they shall never be sick, or in pain any more.

2. *And would not you have your Fathers love; your Mothers Commendation, your Masters good word? Would not you have God and Christ love you? And would you not fain go to Heaven when you die? And live with your godly Parents in Glory, and be happy for ever?*

3. *Whither do you think those Children go, when they dye, that will not do what they are bid, but play the Truant, and Lye, and speak naughty words, and break the Sabbath? Whither do such Children go, do you think? Why, I will tell you, they which Lye, must go to their Father the Devil into everlasting burning; they which never pray, God will pour out his wrath upon them; and when they beg and pray in Hell Fire, God will not forgive them, but there they must lye for ever.*

4. *And are you willing to go to*
Hell

Hell to be burned with the Devil and his Angels? Would you be in the same condition with naughty Chilren? O Hell is a terrible place, that's worse a thousand times than whipping; Gods anger is worse than your Fathers anger; and are you willing to anger God? O Child, this is most certainly true, that all that be wicked, and die so, must be turned into Hell; and if any be once there, there is no coming out again.

5. Would you not do any thing in the World rather than be thrown into Hell Fire? would you not do any thing in the World to get Christ, and grace and glory?

6. Well now, what will you do? will you read this book a little, because your good Mother will make you do it, and because it is a little new Book, but as soon as ever you have done, run away to play, and never think of it?

7. How art thou now affected, poor Child, in the Reading of this Book? Have you shed ever a tear since you begun

begun reading? Have you been by
your self upon your knees, and beg-
ging that God would make you like
these blessed Children? or are you as
you use to be, as careless, and foolish
and disobedient, and wicked as ever?

8. Did you never hear of a little
Child that died? and if other Children
die, why may not you be sick and die?
and what will you do then, Child, if
you should have no grace in your heart,
and be found like other naughty
children?

9. How do you know but that you
may be the next Child that may die?
and where are you then, if you be not
God's Child?

10. Wilt thou tarry any longer,
my dear Child, before thou run into
thy chamber, and beg of God to give
thee a Christ for thy Soul, that thou
mayest not be undone for ever? Wilt
thou get presently into a corner to
weep and pray? Methinks I see that
pretty Lamb begin to weep, and
thinks of getting by himself, and will

as

as well as he can cry unto the Lord, to
make him one of these little ones that
go into the Kingdom of Heaven; Me-
thinks there stands a sweet Child,
and there another, that are resolved
for Christ and for Heaven: Methinks
that little Boy looks as if he had a
mind to learn good things. Methinks
I hear one say, well, I will never tell
a lye more, I will never keep any
naughty Boy company more, they will
teach me to swear, and they will speak
naughty words, they do not love God.
I'le learn my Catechism, and get my
Mother to teach me to pray, and I will
go to weep and cry to Christ, and will
not be quiet till the Lord hath given
me Grace. O that's my brave Child
indeed!

11. But will you not quickly for-
get your promise? are you resolved by
the strength of Christ to be a good
child? Are you indeed? nay, but are
you indeed? Consider: dear child,
God

The Preface.

God calls you to remember your Creator in the dayes of your Youth; and he takes it kindly when little ones come to him, and he loves them dearly; and godly people, especially Parents, and Masters and Mistresses, they have no greater joy, than to see their Children walking in the way of truth.

Now tell me, my pretty dear Child, What will you do? shall I make you a Book? Shall I pray for you, and entreat you? Shall your Good Mother weep over you? And will not you make us all glad, by your turning quickly to the Lord? Shall Christ tell you that he will love you? And will not you love him? Will you strive to be like these Children? I am perswaded, that God intends to do good to the Souls of some little Children by these Papers, because he hath laid it so much upon my heart to pray for them, and over these Papers, and thorow mercy I have already experienced, that something of this nature hath not been in vain: I shall give a
word

word of direction, and so leave you.

1. *Take heed of what you know is naught ; as lying, O that is a grievous fault indeed; and naughty words, and taking the Lords name in vain, and playing upon the Lords Day, and keeping bad company, and playing with ungodly Children : But, if you do go to School with such, tell them that God will not love them, but that the Devil will have them, if they continue to be so naught.*

2. *Do what your Father and Mother bids you, chearfully ; and take heed of doing any thing that they forbid you.*

3. *Be diligent in reading the Scripture, and learning your Catechism ; and what you do not understand, to be sure ask the meaning of.*

4. *Think a little sometimes by your self about God and Heaven, and your Soul, and where you shall go when you die, and what Christ came into the world for.*

5. *And if you have no great mind*

to do thus, but had rather be at play, then think what is it that makes me that I do not care for good things; is this like one of Gods dear Children? I am afraid I am none of God's Child, I feel I do not love to come to Him: O, what shall I do? Either I must be Gods Child or the Devils; O, what shall I do? I would not be the Devils Child for any thing in the world.

6. Then go to your Father or Mother, or some good body, and ask them what thou shalt do to be Gods Child; and tell them that thou art afraid, and that thou canst not be contented, till thou hast got the love of God.

7. Get by thy self, into the Chamber or Garret, and fall upon thy knees, and weep and mourn, and tell Christ thou art afraid that he doth not love thee, but thou would fain have his love; beg of him to give thee his Grace and pardon for thy sins, and that he would make thee his Child: Tell God thou dost not care who don't love thee, if God will but love thee: say to him, Father,

Father, hast thou not a blessing for me, thy poor little Child? Father, hast thou not a blessing for me, even for me? O give a Christ; O give me a Christ; O let me not be undone for ever: thus beg, as for your lives, and be not contented till you have an answer; and do thus every day, with as much earnestness as you can, twice a day at least.

8. Give your self up to Christ: say, dear Jesus, thou didst bid that little Children should be suffered to come unto thee; and Lord, I am come as well as I can, would fain be thy Child: take my heart, and make it humble, and meek, and sensible, and obedient: I give my self to thee, dear Jesus, do what thou wilt with me, so that thou wilt but love me, and give me thy grace and glory.

9. Get acquainted with godly people, and ask them good questions, and endeavour to love their talk.

10. Labour to get a dear love for Christ; read the History of Christ's
sufferings

sufferings, *and ask the reason of his sufferings*; *and never be contented till you see your need of Christ, and the excellency and use of Christ.*

11. *Hear the most powerful Ministers*; *and read the most searching Books*; *and get your Father to buy you* Mr. White's Book *for little Children*, *and* A Guide to Heaven.

12. *Resolve to continue in well-doing all your dayes*; *then you shall be one of those sweet little ones that Christ will take into his Arms, and bless, and give a Kingdom, Crown and Glory to. And now dear Children, I have done, I have written to you, I have prayed for you*; *but what you will do, I can't tell. O Children, if you love me, if you love your Parents, if you love your Souls; if you would scape Hell Fire, and if you would live in Heaven when you dye, do you go and do as these good Children*; *and that you may be your Parents joy, your Countreys honour, and live in Gods fear, and dye in his love, is the prayer of your dear Friend.* J. Janeway:

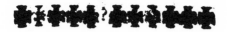

A
TOKEN
FOR
CHILDREN.

EXAMPLE I.

*Of one eminently converted be-
tween Eight and Nine years
old, with an account of her
Life and Death.*

MRS. *Sarah Howley*, when
she was between eight and
nine years old, was carried by her
Friends

Friends to hear a Sermon, where the
Minister Preached upon *Matthew*
11. 30. *My yoak is easie, and my bur-
den is light*: In the applying of which
Scripture, this Child was mightily
awakened, and made deeply sensible
of the condition of her Soul, and her
need of a Christ; she wept bitterly
to think what a case she was in;
and went home and got by her self
into a Chamber, and upon her knees
she wept and cryed to the Lord,
as well as she could, which might
easily be perceived by her eyes and
countenance.

2. She was not contented at this,
but she got her little Brother and
Sister into a Chamber with her, and
told them of their condition by
nature, and wept over them, and
prayed with them and for them.

3. After this she heard another
Sermon upon *Prov.* 29. 1, *He that
being often reproved, hardeneth his
heart, shall suddenly be destroyed,
and*

and that without remedy : At which she was more affected than before, and was so exceedingly solicitous about her Soul, that she spent a great part of the night in weeping and praying, and could scarce take any rest day or night for some time together; desiring with all her Soul to escape from everlasting flames, and to get an interest in the Lord Jesus; O what should she do for a Christ! what should she do to be saved!

4. She gave her self much to attending upon the Word Preached, and still continued very tender under it, greatly favouring what she heard.

5. She was very much in secret prayer, as might easily be perceived by those who listened at the Chamber Door, and was usually very importunate, and full of tears.

6. She could scarce speak of sin, or be spoke to, but her heart was

B   ready

ready to melt.

7. She spent much time in reading the Scripture, and a Book called *The best Friend in the worst times*; by which the work of God was much promoted upon her Soul, and was much directed by it how to get acquaintance with God, especially toward the end of that Book. Another Book that she was much delighted with, was Mr. *Swinnocks Christian Mans Calling*, and by this she was taught in some measure to make Religion her business. The *Spiritual Bee* was a great companion of hers.

8. She was exceeding dutiful to her Parents, very loath to grieve them in the least; and if she had at any time (which was very rare) offended them, she would weep bitterly.

9. She abhorred lying, and allowed her self in no known sin.

10. She was very Conscientious

in

in spending of time, and hated idleness, and spent her whole time either in praying, reading, instructing her little Brothers, and working at her Needle, at which she was very ingenious.

11. When she was at School, she was eminent for her diligence, teachableness, meekness and modesty, speaking very little; but when she did, it was usually very spiritual.

12. She continued in this course of Religious Duties for some years together.

13. When she was about fourteen years old, she brake a Vein in her Lungs (as is supposed), and oft did spit blood, yet did a little recover again, but had several dangerous relapses.

14. At the beginning of *January* last she was taken very bad again, in which sickness She was in great distress of Soul. When she was first

B 2   taken

taken, she said, O Mother, pray,
pray, pray, for me, for Satan is so
busie that I cannot pray for my self,
I see I am undone without a Christ,
and a pardon! O I am undone! un-
done to all Eternity!

15. Her Mother knowing how
serious she had been formerly, did
a little wonder that she should be
in such agonies; upon which her
Mother asked her what sin it was
that was so burdensome to her spi-
rit: O Mother, said she, it is not
any particular Sin of Omission or
Commission, that sticks so close to
my Conscience, as the Sin of my na-
ture; without the blood of Christ,
that will damn me.

16. Her Mother asked her what
she should pray for, for her? she
answered, that I may have a saving
knowledg of Sn and Christ; and
that I may have an assurance of
Gods love to my Soul. Her Mo-
ther asked her, why she did speak
　　　　　　　　　　　　　so

ſo little to the Miniſter that came
to her? She anſwered, that it was
her duty with patience and ſilence
to learn of them: and it was exceed-
ing painful to her to ſpeak to any.

17. One time when ſhe fell in-
to a fit, ſhe cried out, O I am go-
ing, I am going: But what ſhall I
do to be ſaved? O what ſhall I do
to be ſaved? Sweet Lord Jeſus, I
will lye at thy feet, and if I periſh,
it ſhall be at the Fountain of thy
mercy.

18. She was much afraid of pre-
ſumption, and dreaded a miſtake
in the matters of her Soul, and
would be often putting up ejaculati-
ons to God, to deliver her from
deceiving her ſelf. To inſtance in
one: Great and mighty God, give
me faith, and true faith, Lord, that
I may not be a fooliſh Virgin, ha-
ving a Lamp and no Oyl.

19. She would many times be
laying hold upon the Promiſes,

and

and plead them in prayer. That
in *Mat.* 11. 28, 29. was much in
her Tongue, and no small relief to
her spirit. How many times would
she cry out, Lord, hast thou not
said, *Come unto me all ye that are wea-*
ry and heavy laden, and I will give
you rest.

20. Another time her Father
bid her be of good cheer, because
she was going to a better Father;
at which she fell into a great passi-
on, and said, but how do I know
that? I am a poor sinner that wants
assurance: O, for assurance! It was
still her Note, O, for assurance!
This was her great, earnest, and
constant request to all that came
to her, to beg assurance for her;
and, poor heart, she would look
with so much eagerness upon them
as if she desired nothing in the
world so much, as that they would
pity her, and help her with their
prayers; never was poor creature
                                    more

more earnest for any thing, than she
was for an assurance, and the Light
of Gods Countenance : O the pite-
ous moan that she would make !
O the agonies that her Soul was
in !

21. Her Mother askt her, if
God should spare her life, how
she would live; truly Mother, said
she, we have such base hearts that
I can't tell; we are apt to promise
great things; when we are sick, but
when we are recovered, we are as
ready to forget our selves, and to
turn again unto folly; but I hope
I should be more careful of my
time and my soul, than I have
been.

22. She was full of natural af-
fection to her Parents, and very
careful least her Mother shouldbe
tired out with much watching.
Her Mother said, how shall I bear
parting with thee, when I have
scarce dryed my eyes for thy Bro-

ther? She answered, The God of
love support and comfort you; it
is but a little while, and we shall
meet in Glory, I hope. She being
very weak, could speak but lit-
tle; therefore her Mother said,
Child, if thou hast any comfort, lift
up thy hand, which she did.

23. The Lords day before that
in which she died, a Kinsman of
hers came to see her, and asking
of her, whether she knew him,
she answered; yes, I know you,
and I desire you would learn to
know Christ: you are young, but
you know not how soon you may
die; and O to die without a Christ,
it is a fearful thing: O redeem
Time, O Time, Time, Time, pre-
cious Time! Being requested by
him not to spend her self: she said,
she would fain do all the good she
could while she lived, and when
she was dead too, if possible; up-
on which account, she desired that
a Ser-

a Sermon might be Preached at the Funeral concerning the preciousness of Time.   O that young ones would now remember their Creatour!

24. Some Ministers that came to her, did with earnestness, beg that the Lord would please to give her some token for good, that she might go off triumphing; and Bills of the same Nature were sent to several Churches.

25. After she had long waited for an answer of their prayers, she said, *Well, I will venture my soul upon Christ.*

26. She carried it with wonderful patience, and yet would often pray that the Lord would give her more patience, which the Lord answered to astonishment; for considering the pains and agonies that she was in, her patience was next to a wonder; Lord, Lord give me patience, said she, that I may

not dishonour thee.

27. Upon Thursday, after long
waiting, great fears, and many
Prayers, when all her Friends
thought she had been past speaking,
to the astonishment of her Friends
she broke forth thus with a very
audible voice, and chearful Coun-
tenance : Lord, thou hast promi-
sed that whosoever comes unto
thee, thou wilt in no wise cast out ;
Lord, I come unto thee, and sure-
ly thou wilt in no wise cast me out.
O so sweet ! O so glorious is Jesus !
O I have the sweet and glorious Je-
sus ; he is sweet, he is sweet, he
is sweet ! O the admirable love of
God in sending Christ ! O free
grace to a poor lost Creature ! And
thus she ran on repeating many of
these things a hundred times over;
but her Friends were so astonished
to see her in this Divine Rapture,
and to hear such gracious words,
and her prayers and desires satisfi-
ed,

ed, that they could not write a quarter of what she spoke.

28. When her soul was thus ravished with the love of Christ, and her tongue so highly engaged in the magnifying of God ; her Father, Brethren, and Sisters , with other of the Family were called , to whom she spake particularly, as her strength would give leave. She gave her Bible as a Legacy to one of her Brothers , and desired him to use that well for her sake , and added to him and the rest , O make use of time to get a Christ for your Souls; spend no time in running up and down in playing ; O get a Christ for your Souls while you are young, remember now your Creator before you come to a sick-bed ; put not off this great work till then, for then you will find it a hard work indeed. I know by experience , the Devil will tell you it is time enough;and ye are young, what

need

need you to be in such haste? You
will have time enough when you
are old. But there stands one
(meaning her Grand-mother) that
stayes behind, and I that am but
ng, am going before her. O
therefore make your Calling and
Election sure, while you are in
health. But I am afraid this will
be but one nights trouble to your
thoughts; but remmember, these are
the words of a dying Sister. O if
you knew how good Christ were!
O if you had but one taste of his
sweetness, you would rather go to
him a thousand times, than stay in
this wicked world. *I would not*
for ten thousand, and ten thousand
worlds part with my interest in Christ.
O how happy am I that am going
to everlasting Joyes! I would not
go back again for twenty thousand
worlds; And will not you strive
to get an interest in Christ?

26. After this, looking upon one
of

of her Fathers Servants, she said,
what shall I do? What shall I do
at that great day, when Christ shall
say to me, *Come thou Blessed of*
my Father inherit the Kingdom pre-
pared for thee? and shall say to the
wicked, *Go thou cursed into the*
Lake that burns for ever: What a
grief is it to me to think that I shall
see any of my friends that I knew
upon Earth turned into that Lake
that burns for ever! O that word
for ever! Remember that for ever;
I speak these words to you, but
they are nothing, except God speak
to you too. O pray, pray, pray,
that God would give you grace!
and then she prayed, O Lord finish
thy work upon their Souls. It will
be my comfort to see you in glory;
but it will be your everlasting hap-
piness.

30. Her Grandmother told her
she spent her self too much; she
said, I care not for that, if I could
do

do any Soul good. O with what
vehemency, did she speak, as if her
heart were in every word she spoke.

31 She was full of Divine Sen-
tences, and almost all her discourse
from the first to the last in the time
of her sickness, was about her Soul,
Christs sweetness, and the Souls of
others, in a word, like a continued
Sermon.

32. Upon *Friday*, after she had
had such lively discoveries of Gods
love, she was exceeding desirous to
die, and cryed out, Come Lord Je-
sus, come quickly, conduct me to
thy Tabernacle; I am a poor crea-
ture without thee: but Lord Jesus,
my soul longs to be with thee: O
when shall it be? Why not now,
dear Jesus? Come Lord Jesus, come
quickly; but why do I speak thus?
Thy time dear Lord is the best; O
give me patience.

33. Upon *Saturday* she spoke ve-
ry little (being very drowsie) yet
now

now and then she dropt these words,
How long sweet Jesus, finish thy
work sweet Jesus, come away sweet
dear Lord Jesus, come quickly; sweet
Lord help, come away, now, now
dear Jesus, come quickly; Good
Lord give patience to me to wait
thy appointed time; Lord Jesus
help me, help me, help me. Thus
at several times (when out of her
sleep) for she was asleep the greatest
part of the day.

34. Upon the Lords Day she
scarce spoke any thing, but much
desired that Bills of Thanksgiving
might be sent to those who had for-
merly been praying for her, that
they might help her to praise God
for that full assurance that he had
given her of his love; and seemed
to be much swallowed up with the
thoughts of Gods free love to her
Soul. She oft commended her spi-
rit into the Lords hands, and the
last words which she was heard to
                              speak,

speak, were these, Lord help,
Lord Jesus help, Dear Jesus, Blessed
Jesus---- And thus upon the Lords
Day, between Nine and Ten of the
Clock in the Forenoon, she slept
sweetly in Jesus, and began an
everlasting Sabbath, *February* 19.
1670.

EXAMPLE II.

Of a Child that was admirably affect-
ed with the things of God, when he
was between two and three years
Old, with a brief account of his Life
and Death.

1. A Certain little Child, whofe
Mother had dedicated him
to the Lord in the womb : when he
could not fpeak plain , would be
crying after God , and was greatly
defirous to be taught good things.

2. He could not endure to be put
to Bed without family duty , but
would put his Parents upon duty ,
and would with much devotion
kneel down , and with great pati-
ence and delight continue till duty
was at an end, without the leaft ex-
preffion of being weary ; and he fee-
med never fo well pleafed, as when
he was engaged in duty.

3. He

3. He could not be satisfied with Family-duty, but he would be oft upon his knees by himself in one corner or other.

4. He was much delighted in hearing the word of God either read or preached.

5. He loved to go to School that he might learn something of God, and would observe and take great notice of what he had read, and come home and speak of it with much affection; and he would rejoyce in his book, and say to his Mother, O Mother, I have had a sweet lesson to day, will you please to give me leave to fetch my book that you may hear it?

6. As he grew up, he was more and more affected with the things of another world, so that if we had not received our information from one that is of undoubted fidelity, it would seem incredible.

7. He quickly learned to read
the

the Scriptures, and would, with great Reverence, Tenderneſs and groans read, till tears and ſobs were ready to hinder him.

8. When he was at ſecret prayer, he would weep bitterly.

9. He was wont oftentimes to complain of the naughtineſs of his heart, and ſeemed to be more grieved for the Corruption of his Nature than for any actual ſin.

10. He had a vaſt Underſtanding in the things of God, even next to a wonder, for one of his age.

11. He was much troubled for the wandrings of his thoughts in duty, and that he could not keep his heart alway fixed upon God, and the work he was about, and his affections conſtantly raiſed.

12. He kept a watch over his heart, and obſerved the workings of his Soul, and would complain that they were ſo vain and fooliſh, and ſo little buſied about ſpiritual things. 13. Al

13. As he grew up, he grew daily in knowledg and experience; and his carriage was so heavenly, and his discourse so excellent and experimental, that it made those which heard it, even astonished.

14. He was exceeding importunate with God in duty, and would plead with God at a strange rate, and use such arguments in prayer that one would think it were impossible should ever enter into the heart of a Child; he would beg and expostulate and weep so, that sometimes it could not be kept from the ears of Neighbours; so that one of the next house was forced to cry out, the prayers and tears of that Child in the next house will sink me to Hell, because by it he did condemn his neglect of prayer, and his slight performance of it.

15. He was very fearful of wicked company, and would oft beg of God

God to keep him from it, and that he might never be pleased in them that took delight in displeasing of God: And when he was at any time in the hearing of their wicked words, taking the Lords Name in vain, or swearing, or any filthy word, it would even make him tremble, and ready to go home and weep.

16. He abhorred lying with his Soul.

17. When he had committed any fault, he was easily convinced of it, and would get in some corner and secret place, and with tears beg pardon of God, and strength against such a sin. He had a friend that oft watched him, and listned at his Chamber-door, from whom I received this Narrative.

18. When he had been asked, whether he would commit such a sin again, he would never promise absolutely, because he said his heart
was

was naught; but he would weep,
and say, he hoped by the grace of
God he should not.

19. When he was left at home
alone upon the Sabbath days, he
would be sure not to spend any part
of the day in Idleness and Play, but
be busied in praying, Reading in
the Bible, and getting of his Cate-
chism.

20. When other Children were
playing, he would many a time and
oft be praying.

21. One day a certain person
was discoursing with him about
the Nature, Offices, and Excellency
of Christ, and that he alone can
satisfie for our sins, and merit ever-
lasting life for us, and about other
of the great Mysteries of Redempti-
on: he seemed savingly to under-
stand them, and was greatly delight-
ed with the discourse.

22. One speaking, concerning
the Resurrection of the Body, he
did

did acknowledg it ; but that the
same weak body that was buried in
the Church-yard , should be raised
again, he thought very strange,
but with Admiration yielded, that
nothing was impossible to God ;
and that very day he was taken sick
unto death.

23. A Friend of his asked him
whether he were willing to dye
when he was first taken sick ; he
answered, no; because he was a-
fraid of his state as to another
world : Why Child, said the other,
thou didst pray for a new Heart,
for an humble, and a sincere Heart,
and I have heard thee; didst thou
not pray with all thy heart ? I hope
I did, said he.

24. Not long after, the same
person asked him again, whether
he were willing to die ? He answe-
red, now I am willing, for I shall go
to Christ.

25. One asked him what should
become

become of his Sister, if he should die and leave her ? He answered, the will of the Lord must be done,

26. He still grew weaker and weaker, but carried it with a great deal of sweetness and patience, waiting for his change ; and at last did chearfully commit his Spirit unto the Lord , and calling upon the Name of the Lord , and saying, Lord Jesus, Lord Jesus, —— In whose bosome he sweetly slept , dying as I remember, when he was about five or six years old.

Ex-

EXAMPLE III.

*Of a little Girl that was wrought up-
on, when she was between four and
five years old; with some account of
her holy life and triumphant death.*

1. **M**Ary A. When she was be-
tween four and five years
old, was greatly affected in hear-
ing the word of God, and became
very solicitous about her Soul and
everlasting condition, weeping bit-
terly to think what would become
of her in another World, ask-
ing strange questions concerning
God and Christ, and her own soul:
so that this little *Mary*, before she
was full five years old, seemed to
mind the one thing needful, and to
choose the better part, and sat at
the feet of Christ many a time and
oft with tears.

2. She was wont to be much in

C   secret

secret duty, and many times come off
from her knees with tears.

3. She would chuse such times
and places for secret duty, as might
render her less observed by others,
and did endeavour what possibly
she could to conceal what she was
doing when she was engaged in se-
cret duty.

4. She was greatly afraid of hy-
pocrisie, and of doing any thing to
be seen of men, and to get commen-
dation and praise ; and when she
hath heard one of her Brothers say-
ing, that he had been by himself at
prayer, she rebuked him sharply, and
told him how little such prayers
were like to profit him, and that
was little to his praise to pray like
a hypocrite, and to be glad that a-
ny should know what he had been
doing.

5. Her Mother being full of sor-
row after the death of her Hus-
band , this Child came to her Mo-
ther

ther, and askt her why she wept
so exceedingly? her Mother an-
swered, she had cause enough to
weep, because her Father was dead:
No, dear Mother, said the Child,
you have no cause to weep so much,
for God is a good God still to you.

6. She was a dear lover of faith-
ful Ministers. One time after she
had been hearing of Mr. *Whitaker*,
she said I love that man dearly for
the sweet words that he speaks con-
cerning Christ.

7. Her Book was her delight, and
what she did read she loved to make
her own, and cared not for passing
over what she learned without ex-
traordinary observations and under-
standing; and many times she was
so strangely affected in reading of
the Scriptures, that she would burst
out into tears, and would hardly
be pacified, so greatly was she taken
with Christs sufferings, the zeal of
Gods Servant, the danger of a

na-

natural state.

8. She would complain often-times of the corruption of her nature, of the hardness of her heart, that she could repent no more thorowly, and be no more humble and grieved for her sins against a good God; and when she did thus complain, it was with abundance of tears.

9. She was greatly concerned for the souls of others, and grieved to think of the miserable condition that they were in; upon this account, when she could handsomly, she would be putting in some pretty sweet word for Christ; but above all, she would do what she could to draw the hearts of her brethren and sisters after Christ; and there was no small hopes, that her example and good counsel did prevail with some of them when they were very young to get into corners to pray, to ask very gracious

*

questi

queſtions about the things of God.

10. She was very conſcientious in keeping the Sabbath, ſpending the whole time either in reading or praying, or learning her Cate-chiſm, or teaching her Brethren and Siſters. One time when ſhe was left at home upon the Lords day, ſhe got ſome other little chil-dren, together with her brothers and ſiſters, and inſtead of playing (as other naughty children uſe to do) ſhe told them, that that was the Lords day, and that they ought to remember that day to keep it holy; and then ſhe told them how it was to be ſpent in religious exeiciſes all the day long, except ſo much as was to be taken up in the works of neceſſity and mercy; then ſhe pray-ed with them her ſelf, and among other things begged, that the Lord would give grace and wiſdom to them little Children, that they might know how to ſerve him as

one

one of the little ones in the company with her, told afterwards.

11. She was a Child of a strange tenderness and Compassion to all, full of Bowels and Pity: whom she could not help, she would be ready to weep over; especially if she saw her Mother at any time troubled, she would quickly make her sorrows her own, and weep for her and with her.

12. When her Mother had been somewhat solicitous about any worldly thing, she would, if she could possible, put her off from her care one way or other. One time she told her, O Mother, grace is better than that (meaning something her Mother wanted) I had rather have grace and the love of Christ, than any thing in the world.

13. This Child was often musing and busied in the thoughts of her everlasting Work; witness that strange question, O what are they doing

doing which are already in Heaven? And she seemed to be hugely defirous to be among them that were praifing, loving, delighting in God, and ferving of him without fin. Her language was fo ftrange about fpiritual matters, that fhe made many excellent Chriftians to ftand amazed, as judging it fcarce to be paralell'd.

14. She took great delight in reading of the Scripture, and fome p.rt of it was more fweet to her than her appointed food; fhe would get feveral choice Scriptures by heart, and difcourfe of them favourly, and apply them futably.

15. She was not altogether a ftranger to other good Books, but would be reading of them with much affection; and where fhe might, fhe noted the Books particularly, obferving what in the reading did moft warm her heart, and

the was ready upon occafion to improve it.

16. One time a woman coming into the houfe in a great paffion, fpoke of her condition, as if none were like hers, and it would never be otherwife; the Child faid, it were a ftrange thing to fay when its night, it will never be day again.

17. At another time a near Relation of hers being in fome ftreights made fome complaint, to whom fhe faid, I have heard Mr. *Carter* fay, A man may go to Heaven without a Penny in his Purfe; but not without Grace in his heart.

18. She had an extraordinary love to the people of God; and when fhe faw any that fhe thought feared the Lord, her heart would e'n leap for joy.

19. She loved to be much by her felf, and would be greatly grieved if fhe were at any time deprived of a coveniency for fecret duty; fhe
could

could not live without constant addreſs to God in ſecret; and was not a little pleaſed when ſhe could go into a corner to pray and weep.

20. She was much in praiſing God, and ſeldom or never complained of any thing but ſin.

21. She continued in this courſe of praying and praiſing of God, and great dutifulneſs and ſweetneſs to her *Parents*, and thoſe that taught her any thing; yea, ſhe did greatly encourage her Mother while ſhe was a Widow, and deſired that the abſence of a Husband might in ſome meaſure be made up by the dutifulneſs and holineſs of a Child. She ſtudied all the ways that could be to make her Mothers life ſweet.

22. When ſhe was between Eleven and Twelve years old, ſhe ſickned, in which ſhe carried it with admirable patience and ſweetneſs, and did what ſhe could with Scrip-

ture

ture arguments to support and en-
courage her Relations to part with
her that was going to Glory, and
to prepare themselves to meet her in
a blessed Eternity.

23. She was not many days sick
before she was marked; which she
first saw her self, and was greatly
rejoyced to think that she was
marked out for the Lord, and was
now going apace to Christ. She
called to her Friends, and said, I
am marked, but be not troubled,
for I know I am marked for one of
the Lords own. One asked her
how she knew that? She answe-
red; the Lord hath told me that I
am one of his dear Children. And
thus she spake with a holy confi-
dence in the Lords love to her soul,
and was not in the least daunted
when she spake of her death; but
seemed greatly delighted in the ap-
prehension of her nearness to her
Fathers house. And it was not
                                    long

long before she was filled with joy unspeakable in believing.

24. When she just lay a dying, her Mother came to her and told her she was sorry that she had reproved and corrected so good a child so oft. O Mother, said she, speak not thus, I bless God, now I am dying, for your reproofs and corrections too; for it may be, I might have gone to Hell, if it had not been for your reproofs and corrections.

25. Some of her Neighbours coming to visit her, asked her if she would leave them? She answered them, if you serve the Lord, you shall come after me to glory.

26. A little before she died, she had a great conflict with Satan, and cried out, I am none of his; her Mother seeing her in trouble, asked her what was the matter? She answered, Satan did trouble me, but now I thank God all is well, I

know

know I am none of his, but Chrifts.

27. After this, fhe had a great
fenfe of Gods love , and a glorious
fight , as if fhe had feen the very
Heavens open, and the Angels come
to receive her ; by which her heart
was filled with joy, and her tongue
with praife.

28. Being defired by the ftanders
by to give them a particular accoûnt
of what fhe faw: fhe anfwered,
you fhall know hereafter ; and fo
in an extafie of joy and holy tri-
umph , fhe went to Heaven, when
fhe was about Twelve years old.
Hallelujah.

A

A Fourth Example of a Child that began to look towards Heaven when she was about four years old, with some observable passages in her Life and at her Death.

1. A Certain little Child, when she was about four years old, had a conscientious sense of her duty towards her Parents, because the Commandment saith, *Honour thy Father and thy Mother:* And though she had little advantage of education, she carried it with the greatest reverence to her Parents imaginable, so that she was no small credit as well as comfort, to them.

2. It was no unusual thing for her to weep if she saw her Parents troubled, though her self had not been the occasion of it.

3. When she came from School, she would with grief and abhorrency

rency say, that other Children had
sinned against God by speaking
grievous words, which were so bad
that she durst not speak them again.

4. She would be often times ad-
miring of Gods mercy for so much
goodness to her rather than to o-
thers; that she saw some begging,
others blind, some crooked, and
that she wanted nothing that was
good for her.

5. She was many a time and of-
ten in one hole or other in tears up-
on her knees.

6. This poor little thing would
be ready to counsel other little chil-
dren how they ought to serve God,
and putting them upon getting by
themselves to pray; and hath been
known when her friends have been
abroad, to have been teaching Chil-
dren to pray, especially upon the
Lords Day.

7. She very seriously begged the
Prayers of others, that they would
remem-

remember her, that the Lord would give her Grace.

8. When this Child saw some that were laughing, who she judged to be very wicked; She told them, that she feared that they had little reason to be so merry. They asked whether one might not laugh? She answered, no indeed till you have grace, they who are wicked have more need to cry than to laugh.

9. She would say, that it was the duty of Parents, Masters and Mistresses, to reprove (those under their charge) for sin, else God will meet with them.

10. She would be very attentive when she read the Scriptures, and be much affected with them.

11. She would by no means be perswaded to prophane the Lords Day, but would spend it in some good Duties.

12. When she went to School,

it

it was willingly and joyfully, and she was very teachable and exemplary to other children.

13. When she was taken sick, one asked her whether she were willing to die? She answered, Yes, if God would pardon her sins. Being asked how her sins should be pardoned? She answered; through the blood of Christ.

14. She said, she did believe in Christ, and desired, and longed to be with him, and did with a great deal of chearfulness give up her soul.

There were very many observable passages in the Life and Death of this Child, but the hurry and grief that her friends were in, buryed them.

The Fifth Example of the pious Life and joyful Death of a Child which dyed when he was about twelve years old. 1632.

1. CHarles Bridgman had no sooner learned to speak, but he betook himself to prayer.

2. He was very prone to learn the things of God.

3. He would be sometimes teaching them their duty that waited upon him.

4. He learned by heart many good things before he was well fit to go to School: and when he was set to School, he carried it so, that all that observed him either did or might admire him. O the sweet nature, the good disposition, the sincere Religion which was in this Child!

5. When he was at School, what was it that he desired to learn,

but

but Chrift and him crucified.

6. So religious and favoury were his words, his actions fo upright, his devotion fo hearty, his fear of God fo great, that many were ready to fay, as they did of *John, What manner of Child fhall this be?*

7. He would be much in reading the holy Scriptures.

8. He was defirous of more fpiritual knowledg, and would be oft asking very ferious and admirable queftions.

9. He would not ftir out of doors before he had poured out his Soul to the Lord.

11. When he eat any thing, he would be fure to lift up his heart unto the Lord for a bleffing upon it; and when he had moderately refrefhed himfelf by eating, he would not forget to acknowledg Gods goodnefs in feeding of him.

12. He would not lye down in his bed till he had been upon his knees.

knees; and when sometimes he had forgotten his duty, he would quickly get out of his bed, and kneeling down upon his bare knees, covered with no Garment but his Linings, ask God forgiveness for that sin.

13. He would rebuke his Brethren if they were at any time too hasty at their meals, and did eat without asking a blessing; his check was usually this; dare you do thus? God be merciful unto us, this bit of bread might choak us.

14. His sentences were wise and weighty, and well might become some ancient Christian.

15. His sickness was a lingring disease, against which, to comfort him, one tells him of possessions that must fall to his portion; and what are they, said he? I had rather have the Kingdom of Heaven than a thousand such inheritances.

16. When he was sick, he seemed
ed

ed much taken up with Heaven, and asked very serious questions about the nature of his soul.

17. After he was pretty well satisfied about that, he enquired how his soul might be saved; the answer being made, by the applying of Christs merits by faith; he was pleased with the answer, and was ready to give any one that should desire it, an account of his hope.

18. Being asked whether he had rather live or dye, he answered, I desire to dye, that I may go to my Saviour.

19. His pains encreasing upon him, one asked him whether he would rather still endure those pains, or forsake Christ? Alas, said he, I know not what to say, being but a Child, for these pains may stagger a strong man; But I will strive to endure the best that I can. Upon this he called to mind that Martyr *Thomas Bilney*; who being

being in prifon, the night before his burning put his finger into the candle, to know how he could endure the fire. O (faid the Child) had I lived then, I would have run through the fire to have gone to Chrift.

20. His ficknefs lafted long, and at leaft three dayes before his death he prophefied his departure, and not only that he muft dye, but the very day. On the Lords day, faid he, look to me; neither was this a word of courfe, which you may guefs by his often repetition, every day asking, till the day came indeed, what, is Sunday come? At laft the lookt-for day came on; and no fooner had the Sun beautified that morning with its light, but he falls into a trance; his eyes were fixed, his face cheerful, his lips fmiling, his hands and face clafped in a Bow, as if he would have received fome bleffed Angel that were at

hand

hand to receive his foul: but he comes to himself, and tells them how he faw the fweeteft body that ever eyes beheld, who bid him be of good cheer, for he muft prefently go with him.

21. One that ftood near him, as now fufpecting the time of his diffolution nigh, bid him fay, Lord into thy hands I commend my fpirit, which is thy due ; for why? thou haft redeemed it, O Lord my God moft true.

22. The laft words which he fpake, were exactly thefe ; Pray, pray, pray, nay yet pray, and the more Prayers, the better all profpers ; God is the beft Phyfitian, into his hands I commend my fpirit, O Lord Jefus receive my foul : Now clofe mine eyes : Forgive me Father, Mother, Brother, Sifter, all the World. Now I am well, my pain is almoft gone, my joy is at hand, Lord have mercy

on

on me. O Lord receive my Soul un-
to thee. And thus he yielded his
Spirit up unto the Lord, when he
was about twelve years old.

*This Narrative was taken out of
Mr. Ambrose his Life's Lease.*

The

*The sixth Example of a poor Child
   that was awakened when she was
   about five years old.*

1. A Certain very poor Child
      that had a very bad Fa-
ther, but it was to be hoped a very
good Mother, was by the Provi-
dence of God brought to the sight
of a godly friend of mine, who upon
the first sight of the Child, had a
great pity for him, and took an
affection to him, and had a mind to
bring him up for Christ.

2. At the first he did with great
sweetness and kindness allure the
Child, by which means it was not
long before he got a deep interest
in the heart of the Child, and he
began to obey him with more readi-
ness than Children usually do their
Parents.

3. By this a Door was opened
for a farther work, and he had a·

greater advantage to inſtill ſpiritual Principles into the ſoul of the Child, which he was not wanting in, as the Lord gave opportunity, and the Child was capable of.

4. It was not long before the Lord was pleaſed to ſtrike in with the ſpiritual Exhortations of this good man, ſo that the Child was brought to a liking of the things of God.

5. He quickly learnt a great part of the Aſſemblies Catechiſm by heart, and that before he could read his Primmer within Book ; and he took a great delight in learning his Catechiſm.

6. He was not only able to give a very good account of his Cate-chiſm, but he would anſwer ſuch queſtions as are not in the Cate-chiſm, with greater underſtanding than could be expected of one of his age.

7. He took great delight in diſ-
D course

coursing about the things of God; and when my Friend had been either praying or reading, expounding or repeating of Sermons, he seemed very attentive, and ready to receive the truths of God, and would with incredible gravity, diligence, and affection, wait till duties were ended, to the no small joy and admiration of them which observed him.

8. He would ask very excellent questions, and discourse about the condition of his soul and heavenly things, and seemed mightily concerned what should become of his soul when he should dye, so that his discourse made some Christians even to stand astonished.

9. He was greatly taken with the great kindness of Christ in dying for sinners, and would be in tears at the mention of them; and seemed at a strange rate to be affected with the unspeakable love of Christ.

10. When

10. When no body hath been speaking to him, he would burst out into tears ; and being asked the reason, he would say, that the very thoughts of Chrifts love to finners in fuffering for them, made him that he could not but cry.

11. Before he was fix years old, he made confcience of a fecret duty ; and when he prayed, it was with fuch extraordinary meltings, that his eyes have looked red and fore with weeping by himfelf for his fin.

12. He would be putting of Chriftians upon fpiritual difcourfe vvhen he favv them, and feemed little fatisfied ; unlefs they vvere talking of good things.

13. Its evident, That this poor Childs thoughts vvere very much bufied about the things of another vvorld, for he vvould oftentimes be fpeaking to his Bed-fellovv at mid-night, about the matter of his

D 2   Soul ;

foul; and when he could not fleep, he would take heavenly conference to be fweeter than his appointed reft. This was his ufual cuftome, and thus he would provoke and put forward an experienced Chriftian to fpend waking hours in talk of God and the everlafting reft.

14. Not long after this, his good Mother died, which went very near his heart, for he greatly honoured his Mother.

15. After the death of his Mother, he would often repeat fome of the promifes that are made unto Fatherlefs Children, efpecially that in Exod. 22. 22. *Ye fhall not afflict any Widow or the Fatherlefs Child; if thou afflict them in any wife, and they cry at all unto me, I will furely hear their cry.* ———— Thefe words he would often repeat with tears, and fay, I am Fatherlefs and Motherlefs upon Earth, yet if any wrong me, I have a Father in Heaven who

will

will take my part ; to him I commit my felf, and in him is all my truft.

16: Thus he continued in a courfe of holy duties, living in the fear of God, and fhewed wonderful grace for a Child, and died fweetly in the Faith of Jefus.

My friend is a judicious Chriftian of many years experience, who was no ways related to him, but a conftant eye and ear-witnefs of his godly life, and honourable and chearful death, from whom I received this information.

EXAMPLE VII.

Of a notorious wicked child, who was taken up from begging, and admirably converted; with an account of his holy Life and joyful Death, when he was nine years old.

1. A Very poor Child of the Parish of *Newington-Butts* came begging to the door of a dear Christian friend of mine, in a very lamentable case, so filthy and nasty, that he would even have turned ones stomack to have looked on him: But it pleased God to raise in the heart of my friend, a great pity and tenderness towards this poor child, so that in Charity he took him out of the streets, whose Parents were unknown, who had nothing at all in him to commend him to any ones Charity, but his misery. My friend eying the

glory

glory of God, and the good of the immortal soul of this wretched Creature, discharged the Parish of the Child, and took him as his own, designing to bring him up for the Lord Christ. A noble piece of Charity! And that which did make the kindness far the greater was, that there seemed to be very little hopes of doing any good upon this Child, for he was a very Monster of wickedness, and a thousand times more miserable and vile by his sin, than by his poverty. He was running to Hell as soon as he could go, and was old in naughtiness when he was young in years; and one shall scarce hear of one so like the Devil in his infancy, as this poor Child was. What sin was there (that his age was capable of) that he did not commit? What by the corruption of his Nature, and the abominable example of little beggar boyes, he was ar-

D 4   rived

rived to a strange pitch of impiety.
He would call filthy Names, take
Gods Name in vain, curse and
swear, and do almost all kind of
mischief; and as to any thing of
God, worse than an Heathen.

2. But his sin and misery was
but a stronger motive to that graci-
ous man to pity him, and to do all
that possibly he could to pluck this
fire-brand out of the fire; and it
was not long before the Lord was
pleased to let him understand that
he had a design of everlasting kind-
ness upon the Soul of this poor
child : for no sooner had this good
man taken this creature into his
house, but he prays for him, and
labours with all his might to con-
vince him of his miserable conditi-
on by Nature, and to teach him
something of God, the worth of
his own Soul, and that Eternity of
Glory or Misery that he was born
to; and blessed be Free-grace, it
was

was not long before the Lord was
pleafed to let him underftand, that
it was himfelf which put it into his
heart to take in this Child, that he
might bring him up for Chrift. The
Lord foon ftruck in with his godly
inftructions, fo that an amazing
change was feen in the Child, in a
few weeks fpace he was foon con-
vinced of the evil of his ways; no
more news now of his calling of
Names, Swearing, or Curfing;
no more takirg of the Lords Name
in vain; now he is civil, and re-
fpectful, and fuch a ftrange alte-
ration waswrougt tin the child,that
all the Parifh that rung of his vil-
lany before, was now ready to
talk of his reformation; his com-
pany, his talk, his imployment is
now changed, and he is like ano-
ther creature; fo that the glory of
Gods Free-grace began already to
fhine in him.

3. And this change was not on-

ly an eternal one, and to be difcern-
ed abroad , but he would get by
himfelf, and weep and mourn bit-
terly for his horrible wicked life, as
might eafily be perceived by them
that lived in the houfe with him.

4. It was the great care of his
godly Mafter to ftrike in with thofe
convictions which the Lord had
made, and to improve them all he
could ; and he was not a little glad
to fee that his labour was not in
vain in the Lord ; he ftill experien-
ces that the Lord doth carry on
his own work mightily upon the
heart of the Child, he is ftill more
and more broken under a fenfe of
his undone ftate by nature; he is oft
in tears and bemoaning his loft and
miferable condition. When his
Mafter did fpeak of the things of
God, he liftened earneftly, and took
in with much greedinefs and affecti-
on what he was taught.? Seldom
was there any difcourfe about Soul-
mat-

matters in his hearing, but he heard it as if it were for his life, and would weep greatly.

5. He would after his Master had been speaking to him or others of the things of God, go to him, and question with him about them, and beg of him to instruct and teach him further, and to tell him those things again, that he might remember and understand them better.

6. Thus he continued seeking after the knowledg. of God and Christ, and practising holy duties, till the sickness came into the house, with which the child was smitten; at his first sickning, the poor child vvas greatly amazed and afraid, and though his pains were great, and the distemper very tedious, yet the sense of his sin, and the thoughts of the miserable condition that he feared his soul vvas still in, made his trouble ten times greater; he was in grievous agonies of spirit, and

is

his former sins stared him in the face, and made him tremble; the poison of Gods Arrows did even drink up his spirits; the sense of sin and wrath was so great, that he could not tell what in the world to do; the weight of Gods displeasure, and the thoughts of lying under it to all eternity, did even break him to pieces, and he did cry out very bitterly, what should he do? he was a miserable sinner, and he feared that he should go to Hell; his sins had been so great and so many that there was no hopes for him. He was not by far so much concerned for his life, as for his Soul, what would become of that for ever. Now the plague upon his body seemed nothing to that which was in his soul.

7. But in this great distress the Lord was pleased to send one to take care for his Soul, who urged to him the great and precious promises which were made to one in

his

his condition, telling him that there was enough in Chrift for the chiefeft of finners, and that he came to feek and fave fuch a loft creature as he was. But this poor Child found it a very difficult thing for him to believe that there was any mercy for fuch a dreadful finner as he had been.

8. He was made to cry out of himfelf, not only for his fwearing and lying, and other outwardly notorious fins; but he was in great horrour for the fin of his Nature, for the vilenefs of his heart, and original corruption; under it he was in fo great anguifh, that the trouble of his fpirit made him in a great meafure to forget the pains of his body.

9. He did very particularly confefs and bewail his fins with tears; and fome fins fo fecret that none in the world could charge him with.

10. He would condemn himfelf

for

or fin, as deferving to have no mercy, though that there was not a greater finner in all *London* than himfelf, and he abhorred himfelf as the vileft creature he knew.

11. He did not only pray much with ftrong cries and tears himfelf, but he begged the prayers of Chriftians for him.

12. He would ask Chriftians, whether they thought there were any hopes for him, and would beg of them to deal plainly with him, for he was greatly afraid of being deceived.

13. Being informed how willing and ready the Lord Chrift was to accept of poor finners upon their repentance and turning, and being counfelled to venture himfelf upon Chrift for mercy and falvation, he faid he would fain caft himfelf upon Chrift, but he could not but wonder how Chrift fhould be willing to dye for fuch a vile wretch as he was;

and

and he found it one of the hardeſt things in the world to believe.

14. But at laſt it pleaſed the Lord to give him ſome ſmall hopes that there might be mercy for him, for he had been the chiefeſt of ſinners ; and he was made to lay a little hold upon ſuch promiſes, as that, *Come unto me all ye that are weary and heavy laden, and I will give you reſt.* But O how did this poor boy admire and bleſs God for the leaſt hopes ! How highly did he advance free and rich grace that ſhould pity and pardon him ! and at laſt he was ſo full of praiſe, and admiring of God, ſo that (to ſpeak in the words of a precious man, that was an eye and ear-witneſs) to rhe praiſe and glory of God be it ſpoken, the houſe at that day, for all the ſickneſs in it, was a little lower Heaven, ſo full of joy and praiſe.

15 The Child grew exceeding-
ly

ly in knowledg, experiences, patience, humility, and self-abhorrency, and he thought he could never speak bad enough of himself; the Name that he would call himself by, was a Toad.

16. And though he prayed before, yet now the Lord poured out upon him the Spirit of prayer in an extraordinary manner, for one of his age; so that now he prayed more frequently, more earnestly, more spiritually than ever. O how eagerly would he beg to be washed in the Blood of Jesus; and that the King of Kings, and Lord of Lords, that was over Heaven and Earth, and Sea, would pardon and forgive him all his sins, and receive his Soul into his Kingdom! and what he spoke, it was with so much life and fervour of Spirit, as that it filled the hearers with astonishment and joy.

17. He

17. He had no small sense of the use and excellency of Christ, and such longings and breathings of his Soul after him, that when mention hath been made of Christ, he hath been ready almost to leap out of his bed for joy.

18. When he was told that if he should recover, he must not live as he list; but he must give up himself to Christ, and to be his Child and Servant, to bear his Yoke, and be obedient unto his Laws, and live a holy life, and take his Cross' and suffer mocking and reproach' it may be persecution for his Name sake. Now Child (said one to him) are you willing to have Christ upon such terms? He signified his willingness by the earnestness of his looks and words, and the casting up of his eyes to Heaven, saying, yes, with all my Soul, the Lord helping me, I will do this.

19. Yet he had many doubts
mot

and fears, and was ever and anon
harping upon that, that though he
were willing, yet Christ he feared
was not willing to accept him, be-
cause of the greatness of his sin,
yet his hopes were greater than his
fears.

20. The *Wednesday* before he
died, the Child lay as it were in a
trance for about half an hour, in
which time he thought he saw a
Vision of Angels: When he was
out of his Trance, he was in a little
pett, and asked his Nurse, why
she did not let him go; go, whither
child, said she? why along with
those brave Gentlemen (said he):
but they told me they would come
and fetch me away for all you, upon
Friday next. And he doubled his
words many times, upon *Friday*
next, those brave Gentlemen will
come for me; and upon that day
the Child dyed joyfully.

21. He was very thankful to his Master, and very sensible of his great kindness in taking him up out of the streets when he was a begging, and he admired at the goodness of God, which put it into the mind of a stranger to look upon, and to take such fatherly care of such a pitiful sorry creature as he was. O my dear Mother (said he) and child of God, I hope to see you in Heaven, for I am sure you will go thither. O blessed, blessed be God that made you to take pity upon me, for I might have dyed, and have gone to the Devil, and have been damned for ever, if it had not been for you.

22. The Thursday before he dyed he asked a very godly friend of mine, what he thought of his condition, and whither his soul was now going? for he said he could not still but fear least he should deceive himself with false hopes,

at

at which my friend spoke to him thus, Child, for all that I have endeavoured to hold forth the grace of God in Christ to thy Soul, and given you a warrant from the Word of God, that Christ is as freely offered to you, as to any sinner in the world; if thou art but willing to accept of him, thou mayest have Christ and all that thou dost want, with him; and yet thou givest way to these thy doubtings and fears, as though I told thee nothing but lyes. Thou sayest thou fearest that Christ will not accept of thee; I fear thou art not heartily willing to accept of him. The Child answered, indeed I am: Why then Child, if thou art unfeignedly willing to have Christ, I tell thee he is a thousand times more willing to have thee, and wash thee, and save thee, than thou art to desire it. And now at this time

Christ

Chriſt offers himſelf freely to thee
again; therefore receive him hum-
bly by Faith into thy heart, and
bid him welcome, for he deſerv-
eth it: Upon which words the
Lord diſcovered his love to the
Child, and he gave a kind of a leap
in his bed, and ſnapt his fingers and
thumb together with abundance of
joy, as much as to ſay, Well, yea all
is well, the match is made, Chriſt
is willing, and I am willing too;
and now Chriſt is mine, and I am
his for ever. And from that time
forward, in full joy and aſſurance
of Gods love, he continued ear-
neſtly praiſing God, with deſiring
to die, and be with Chriſt. And
on Friday morning he ſweetly
went to reſt, uſing that very ex-
preſſion, Into thy hands Lord I
commit my ſpirit. He died punc-
tually at that time which he had
ſpoke of, and in which he expected
those

thofe Angels to come to him; he was not much above nine years old when he dyed.

This Narrative I had from a judicious holy man un-related to him, who was an eye and ear-witnefs to all thefe things.

———————————————

FINIS.

A

TOKEN
FOR
CHILDREN.

The Second Part.

BEING

A farther Account of the
Conversion, Holy and ex-
emplary Lives, and Joyful
Deaths of several other
young Children, not published
in **The first Part.**

By *James Janeway*, Minister
of the Gospel.

Psal. 8. 2.

Out of the Mouth of **Babes** *and* **Suck-
lings** *hast thou ordained strength.*

LONDON,

Printed for *D. Newman*, at the
Kings Arms at the Corner of *Grocers
Alley* in the *Poultrey*, 1673.

A

PREFACE

TO THE

READER.

Christian Reader,

IN the former part of my Tokens
for Children, I did in part pro-
mise, that if that piece met with
kind entertainment, it might be fol-
lowed with a second of the same na-
ture. If it did not seem a little to sa-
vour of vanity, I might tell the World
what encouragement I have met with
in this Work; but this I will only say,
that I have met with so much as hath
perswaded me to give this little Book
leave to go abroad into the World. I
am not also ignorant, what Discou-

A 2   rage-

ragement I may meet with from some,
but as long as I am sure I shall not
meet with this, that it's improbable,
if not impossible, that it should save a
Soul; I think the rest may easily be
answered, or warrantably slighted.
But because I am perswaded by some,
that one Example in the former,
(viz. that of a Child that began to be
serious between two and three years old)
was scarce credible, and they did fear
might somewhat prejudice the autho-
rity of the rest, I shall say something
to answer that. They which make
this Objection are either good or bad;
if bad, I expect never to satisfie them,
except I should tell them of a Ro-
mance or a Play, or somewhat that
might suit a carnal mind; it is like
holiness in older persons, is a matter
of contempt and scorn to them, much
more in such as these I mention. The
truth of it is, it is no wonder at all to
me, that the Subjects of Satan should
not be very well pleased with that,
whose design is to undermine the inte-

rest

rest of their great Mister: nothing will satisfie some, except Christ and holiness may be degraded and vilified. But bold sinner hold, never hope it, Heaven shall never be turned into Hell for thy sake, and as for all thy Atheistical Objections, Scoffs and Jeers, they shall ere long be fully answered; and the Hosannah's and Hallelujah's of these Babes shall condemn thy Oaths, Blasphemies, and Jeers, and then thou wilt be silenced, and accept converting Grace turn thy heart quickly, thou wilt for ever rue thy madness and Folly, when it is too late to remedy it.

But if the Persons that make this Objection be godly, I question not but that I may give them reasonable satisfaction.

First, consider who it is that I had that example from. It was one Mrs. Jeofries in Long-Lane in Mary Magdalen Bermondsey Parish, in the County of Surry, a woman of that same in the Church of Christ, for

her

her exemplary Piety., Wisdom, Experience, and singular watchfulness over every punctilio that she speaks; that I question not but that her name is precious to most of the Ministers of London, at least in the Burrough; and as a reverend Divine said, Such a Mother in Israel, her single Testimony about London, is of as much authority almost as any one single Ministers: And having since discoursed this matter with her, she calls God to witness, that she hath spoken nothing but the Truth; only in this she failed, in that she spake not by far so much as she might have done concerning that sweet Babe. I might add, that I have since that, seen a godly gentleman out of the Countrey, that did profess to me, that he had seen as much as that in a little one of the same age, who since that time, I hear; went sweetly to Heaven. Doth not the Reverend Mr. Clark, in his Works, quote a Child of two years old that looked towards Heaven?

Doth

To the Reader.

Doth not credible History acquaint us with a Martyr at seven years old, that was whipped almost to death, and never shed one tear nor complained, and at last had his Head struck off? I do not speak of these as common matters, but record them amongst those stupendious Acts of him that can as easily work Wonders as not. What is too hard for the Almighty? Hath God said he will work no more wonders? I think most of Gods works in the business of Conversion call for Admiration: And I believe that Silence or rather Praise would better become Saints, than questioning the truth of such things; especially where an apparent Injury is thereby done to the Interest of Christ, the Honour of Gods Grace, and the Reputation of so eminent a Saint. I judge this sufficient to satisfie most, as for others I trouble not my self; if I may but promote the interest of Christ, and the Good of Souls, and give up my Account with joy, it's enough. That

the

To the Reader.

the Lord would bless my endeavours to these ends, I beg the prayers of all Saints, and yours also sweet Children that fear the Lord; and that Parents and Masters would assist me with their warm application of these things, and that Children may be their Crown and their Joy, is the Prayer of one that desires to love Christ and little children dearly.

James Janeway,

A
TOKEN
FOR
CHILDREN.

The Second Part.

Example VIII.

Of a Child that was very serious at four years old, with an Account of his comfortable Death when he was twelve years and three weeks old.

1. **I**Ohn Sudlow was born of religious Parents in the County of *Middlesex*, whose great care was to instill spiritual Principles into him as soon as he was capable of understanding of them; whose Endeavours the Lord was pleased to crown with the desired success; so that (to use the expression of a holy man

A 5
con-

concerning him) scarce more could
be expected or desired from so little
a one.

2. When he was scarce able to
speak plain, he seemed to have a
very great awe and reverence of
God upon his spirit, and a strange
sense of the things of another world,
as might easily be perceived by
those serious and admirable questi-
ons which he would be oft asking
of those Christians that he thought
he might be bold with.

3. The first thing that did most
affect him, and made him endea-
vour to escape from the wrath to
come, and to enquire what he
should do to be saved, was the
death of a little Brother; when he
saw him without breath, and not
able to speak or stir, and then car-
ried out of doors, and put into a
pit-hole, he was greatly concerned,
and asked notable questions about
him, but that which was most af-
fecting of himself and others, was
                                        whe-

whether he muſt die too, which being anſwered, it made ſuch a deep impreſſion upon him, that from that time forward he was exceeding ſerious and this was when he was about four years old.

4. Now he is deſirous to know what he might do that he might live in another world, and what he muſt avoid, that he might not die for ever, and being inſtructed by his godly Parents, he ſoon labours to avoid whatſoever might diſpleaſe God; now tell him that any thing was ſinful, and that God would not have him do it, and he is eaſily kept from it, and even at this time of day the apprehenſions of God and Death and Eternity laid ſuch a reſtraint upon him, that he would not for a world have told a Lie.

5. He quickly learned to read exactly, and took ſuch Pleaſure in reading of the Scriptures and his Catechiſm, and other good Books, that it is ſcarce to be parallel'd; he
would

would naturally run to his Book
without bidding, when he came
home from School; and while o-
ther children of his age and ac-
quaintance were playing, he reckon'd
it his Recreation to be doing that
which was good.

6. When he was in coats, he
would be still asking his maid serious
questions, and praying her to teach
him his Catechism or Scriptures, or
some good thing; common Di-
scourse he took no delight in, but
did most eagerly desire to be sucking
in of the knowledge of the things of
God, Christ, his Soul, and another
world.

7. He was hugely taken with the
reading of the Book of Martyrs, and
would be ready to leave his Dinner to
go to his Book.

8. He was exceeding careful of
redeeming and improving of time;
scarce a moment of it, but he would
give an excellent account of the ex-
pence of it; so that this Child
might

might have taught elder perfons,
and will queftionlefs condemn
their idle and unaccountable waft-
ing of thofe precious hours in which
they fhould, as this fweet Child,
have been laying in provifion for
Eternity.

9. He could not endure to read
any thing over flightly, but what-
foever he read he dwelt upon it,
laboured to underftand it through-
ly, and remember it; and what he
could not underftand he would oft
ask his Father or Mother the meaning
of.

10. When any Chriftian friends
have been difcourfing with his Fa-
ther, if they began to talk any thing
about Religion, to be fure they
fhould have his company, and of
his own accord he would leave all
to hear any thing of Chrift, and
creep as clofe to them as he could,
and liften as affectionately though
it were for an hour or two: He
was fcarce ever known to exprefs
the

the least token of weariness while he was hearing any thing that was good, and sometimes when neighbours children would come and call him out, and entice him and beg of him to go with them, he could by no means be perswaded, though he might have had the leave of his Parents, if he had any hopes that any good body would come in to his fathers house.

11. He was very modest whilest any stranger was present, and was loth to ask them any questions, but as soon as they were gone, he would let his father know that there was little said or done but he observed it, and would reflect upon what was past in their discourse, and desire satisfaction in what he could not understand at present.

12. He was a Boy of almost prodigious parts for his age, as will appear by his solid and rational questions; I shall mention but two of many.

13. The

13. The firſt was this, when he was reading by himſelf in *Draiton's* Poems about *Noah's* Flood and the Ark, he askt who built the Ark? it being anſwered that it was likely that *Noah* hired men to help him to build it : And would they (ſaid he) build an Ark to ſave another, and not go into it themſelves?

14. Another queſtion he put was this; Whether had the greater glory Saints or Angels? It being anſwered, that Angels were the moſt excellent of Creatures, and its to be thought their nature is made capable of greater glory than mans. He ſaid he was of another mind, and his reaſon was, becauſe Angels were Servants, and Saints are Children ; and that Chriſt never took upon him the nature of Angels, but he took upon him the nature of Saints, and by his being man he hath advanced human nature above the nature of Angels.

15. By this you may perceive the greatneſs of his parts, and the bent
of

of his thoughts, and thus he conti-
nued for several years together, la-
bouring to get more and more fpi-
ritual knowledge, and to prepare for
an endlefs life.

16.   He was a Child of an excel-
lent fweet-temper, wonderful duti-
ful to his Parents, ready and joyful
to do what he was bid, and by no
means would do any thing to dif-
pleafe them, and if they were at any
time feemingly angry, he would
not ftir from them till they were tho-
rowly reconciled to him.

17.   He was not only good him-
felf, but would do what he could
to make others fo too, efpecially
thofe that were neareft to him; he
was very watchful over his brethren
and Sifters, and would not fuffer
them to ufe any unhandfome words
or to do any unhandfome action, but
he would be putting them upon
that which was Good, and when he
did at any time rebuke them, it
was not Childifhly and flightly, but
                              with

with great gravity and seriousness, as one that was not a little concerned for Gods honour, and the eternal welfare of their Souls.

18. He would go to his Father and Mother with great tenderness and compassion (being far from telling of tales) and beg of them to take more care of the Souls of his brethren and Sisters, and to take heed least they should go on in a sinful Christless state, and prove their sorrow and shame, and go to Hell when they die, and be ruined for ever.

19. He was exceedingly affected with hearing of the Word of God preached, and could not be satisfied except he could carry home much of the substance of what he heard; to this end he quickly got to learn Short-hand, and would give a very pretty account of any Sermon that he heard.

20. He was much engaged in secret Duty, and in reading the Scri-

Scriptures; to be sure morning and evening he would be by himself, and was, no question wrestling with God.

21. He would get choice Scriptures by heart, and was very perfect at his Catechism.

22. The Providences of God were not passed by without considerable observation by him.

23. In the time of the Plague he was exceedingly concerned about his Soul and Everlasting State; very much by himself upon his knees. This Prayer was found written in Short-hand after his Death.

O Lord God and merciful Father, take pitie upon me a miserable Sinner, and strengthen me, O Lord, in thy faith, and make me one of thy glorious Saints in Heaven. O Lord keep me from this poisonous Infection; however not my will but thy will be done, O Lord, on earth as it is in heaven, but O Lord, if thou hast ap-
pointed

pointed me to die by it, O Lord, fit me for death, and give me a good heart to bear up under my afflictions: O Lord God and merciful Father, take pity on me thy child, teach me O Lord thy Word, make me strong in faith. O Lord I have sinned against thee, Lord pardon my sins ; I had been in hell long ago if it had not been for thy mercy ; O Lord, I pray thee to keep my Parents in thy truth, and save them from this Infection, if it be thy will, that they may live to bring me up in the truth : O Lord I pray thee stay this Infection that rageth in this City, and pardon their sins, and try them once more, and see if they will turn unto thee. Save me O Lord from this Infection, that I may live to praise and glorifie thy name, but O Lord if thou hast appointed me to die of it , fit me for death, that I may die with comfort ; and O Lord, I pray thee to help me to bear up under all afflictions, for Christ his sake. Amen.

24. He

24. He was not a little concerned for the whole nation, and begged that God would pardon the sins of the Land, and bring it nearer to himself.

25. About the beginning of *November*, 1665. this sweet Child was smote with the Distemper, but he carried it with admirable patience under the hand of God.

26. These are some of his dying Expressions. —— *The Lord shall be my Physician, for he will cure both Soul and body.*—*Heaven is the best Hospital.* —*It is the Lord, let him do what seemeth good in his eyes.* Again, —*it is the Lord that taketh away my health, but I will say as* Job did, *Blessed be the name of the Lord.* —— *If I should live longer, I should but sin against God.* Looking upon his Father, he said, *If the Lord would but lend me the least finger of his hand to lead me through the dark entry of Death, I will rejoice in him.*

27. When a Minister came to him, amongst other things he spake

some-

somewhat of life. He said, *This is a wicked world, yet it is good to live with my Parents, but it is better to live in heaven.* —

28. An hour and an half before his Death, the same Minister came again to visit him, and asked him, John, *art thou not afraid to die*: He answered, *No, if the Lord will but comfort me in that hour.* But said the Minister, *How canst thou expect Comfort seeing we deserve none?* He answered, *No, if I had my deserts I had been in hell long ago.* But, replied the Minister, *which way dost thou expect Comfort and Salvation, seeing thou art a Sinner.* He answered, *In Christ alone.* — In whom, about an hour and an half after, he fell asleep, saying he would take a long sleep, charging them that were about him not to wake him.

He dyed when he was twelve years three weeks and a day old.

EXAM-

Example IX.

*Of a Child that was very eminent
when she was between 5 and 6 years
old, with some memorable passages
of her life, who died about* 1640.

1. A Nne *Lane* was born of ho-
    nest Parents in *Colebrook* in
the County of *Bucks*, who was no
sooner able to speak plain, and ex-
press any thing considerable of rea-
son, but she began to act as if she
was sanctified from the very womb.

2. She was very solicitous about
her Soul, what would become of it
when she should die, and where
she should live for ever, and what
she should do to be saved, when
she was about five years old.

3. She was wont to be oft ingaged
in secret Prayer, and pouring out of
her Soul in such a manner as is rarely
to be heard of from one of her years.

4. I having occasion to lie at *Cole-
brook* sent for her Father, an old
Dis-

Diſciple, an Iſraelite indeed, and deſired him to give me ſome account of his Experiences, and how the Lord firſt wrought upon him.

5. He gave me this anſwer, that he was of a child ſomewhat civil, honeſt, and as to man harmleſs, but was little acquainted with the power of Religion, till this ſweet Child put him upon a thorow inquiry into the ſtate of his Soul, and would ſtill be begging of him, and pleading with him to redeem his time, and to act with life and vigor in the things of God, which was no ſmall demonſtration to him of the reality of inviſibles, that a very Babe and ſuckling ſhould ſpeak ſo feelingly about the things of God, and be ſo greatly concerned not only about her own ſoul, but about her Fathers too, which was the occaſion of his converſion, and the very thought of it was a quickning to him for thirty years, and he hopes never to wear off the Impreſſions of it from his ſpirit.   6. After

6. After this she (as I remember)
put her Father upon Family duties,
and if at any time he were for any
time out of his shop, she would
find him out, and with much sweet-
ness and humility beg of him to
come home, and to remember the
pretiousness of time, for which we
must all give an account.

7. She was grieved if she saw
any that conversed with her father
if they were unprofitable, unsavoury
or long in their discourse of common
things.

8. Her own Language was the
Language of *Canaan*: how solidly,
profitably and spiritually would
she talk? so that she made good
people take great delight in her com-
pany, and justly drew the admiration
of all that knew her.

9. She could not endure the
company of common children, nor
play, but was quite above all those
things which most Children are ta-
ken with; her business was to be
reading,

reading, praying, difcourfing, about the things of God, and any kind of bufinefs that her age and ftreng h was capable of, idle fhe would n t be by any means.

10. It was the greateft Recreation to her to hear any good people talking about God, Chrift, their Souls, the Scriptures, or any thing that concerned another life.

11. She had a ftrange contempt of the World, and fcorned thofe things which moft are too much pleafed with. She could not be brought to wear any Laces, or any thing that fhe thought fuperfluous.

12. She would be complaining to her parents, if fhe faw any thing in them that fhe judged would not be for the honour of Religion, or fuitable to that condition which the providence of God had fet them in, in the world.

13. This Child was the joy and delight of all the Chriftians thereabouts in thofe times, who was ftill

B   quick-

quickning and raifing of the fpirits
of thofe that talked with her. This
poor Babe was a great help to both
Father and mother, and her memory
is fweet to this day.

14. She continued thus to walk
as a ftranger in the world, and one
that was making haft to a better
place. And after fhe had done a
great deal of work for God and her
own foul, and others too, fhe was
called home to reft, and received in-
to the arms of Jefus before fhe was
ten years old; fhe departed about
1640.

EXample

Example X.

*Of a Child that was awakened when
she was between seven and eight
years old, with some account of her
last hours and triumphant Death.*

1. T**Abitha** **Alder** was the
Daughter of a holy and
Reverend Minister in *Kent*, who
lived near *Gravesend*. She was
much instructed in the holy Scrip-
tures and her Catechism by her
Father and Mother, but there ap-
peared nothing extraordinary in
her till she was between seven and
eight years old.

2. About which time, when she
was sick, one asked her what she
thought would become of her if she
should die? She answered, that
she was greatly afraid that she should
go to hell.

3. Being askt why she was afraid
she should go to hell? She answered,
because she feared that she did not love
God.   B 2   4. Again

4. Again being askt how she did know she did not love God; she replyed, what have I done for God ever since I was born; and besides this, I have been taught, that he that loves God keeps his commandments but I have kept none of them all.

5. Being further demanded if she would not fain love God? She answered, yes with all her heart, if she could, but she found it a hard thing to love one she did not see.

6. She was advised to beg of God a heart to love him: She answered, she was afraid it was too late.

7. Being asked again whether she was not sorry that she could not love God: She answered, yes, but was still afraid it was too late.

8. Upon this, seeing her in such a desponding condition, a dear friend of hers spent the next day in Fasting and prayer for her.

9. After this, that Christian friend askt her how she did now? She answered with a great deal of joy, that now

now she blessed the Lord, she loved the Lord Jesus dearly, she felt she did love him. O, said she, I love him dearly.

10. Why, saith her friend, did you not say yesterday, that you did not love the Lord, and that you could not? What did you mean to speak so strangely? Sure (said she) it was Satan that did put it into my mind: But now I love him, O blessed be God for the Lord Jesus Christ.

11. After this she had a discovery of her approaching Dissolution, which was no small comfort to her. Anon (said she with a holy Triumph) I shall be with Jesus, I am married to him, he is my husband, I am his Bride, I have given my self to him, and he hath given himself to me, and I shall live with him for ever.

12. This strange language made the hearers even stand astonished: but thus she continued for some little time in a kind of extasie of joy admi-

admiring the excellency of Chrift
rejoycing in her interett in him, and
longing to be with him.

13. After a while fome of her
friends ftanding by her, obferved a
more than ordinary earneftnefs and
fixednefs in her countenance; they
faid one to another, look how earneft-
ly fhe looks, fure fhe feeth fomething.

14. One asked what it was fhe
fixed her eyes upon fo eagerly: I
warrant (faith one that was by) fhe
feeth death a coming.

15. No (faid fhe) it is glory that
I fee, 'tis that I fix mine eye upon.

16. One askt her what was glory
like? She anfwered, I can't fpeak
what, but I am going to it; will you
go with me? I am going to glory, O
that all of you were to go with me
to that glory! with which words her
Soul took wing, and went to the
poffeffion of that glory which fhe
had fome believing fight of before.
She died when fhe was betwen 8 and
9 years old, about 1644.

Exam-

Example XI.

*Of a Child that was greatly affected
with the things of God when she
was very young, with an exact
Account of her admirable Carriage upon her Death bed.*

1. Sufanna Bicks was born at Leiden in Holland, *Jan.* 24. 1650.
of very religious Parents, whose
great care was to inftruct and cate-
chife this their Child, and to prefent
her to the Minifters of the place, to be
publickly inftructed and catechifed.

2. It pleafed the Lord to blefs
holy education, the good example
of her Parents and catechifing, to
the good of her Soul, fo that fhe
foon had a true favour and relifh of
what fhe was taught, and made an
admirable ufe of it in a time of
need, as you fhall hear afterwards.

3. She was a Child of great du-
tifulnefs to her Parents, and of a
very fweet humble fpiritual nature,

B 4   and

and not only the truth, but the power and eminency of Religion did shine in her so clearly, that she did not only comfort the hearts of her Parents, but drew the admiration of all that were witnesses of Gods works of love upon her, and may well be proposed as a pattern not only to Children, but to persons of riper years,

4. She continued in a course of Religious Duties for some considerable time, so that her life was more excellent than most Christians, but in her last sickness she excelled her self, and her deportment was so admirable, that partly through wonder and astonishment, and partly through sorrow, many observable things were past by without committing to paper, which deserved to have been written in letters of gold: But take these which follow as some of many which were taken from her dying lips, and first published by religious and judicious Christians
in

in *Dutch*, afterward tranflated into *Scotch*, and with a little alteration of the ftile (for the benefit of *Englifh* Children) brought into this form by me.

5. In the month of *Auguft*, 1664. When the Peftilence raged fo much in *Holland*, this fweet Child was fmitten, and as foon as fhe felt her-felf very ill, fhe was faid to break forth with abundance of fenfe and feeling in thefe following words: *If thy Law were not my delight, I ſhould periſh in my affliction.*

6. Her Father coming to her to encourage her in her ficknefs, faid to her, be of good comfort my Child for the Lord will be near to thee and us, under this heavy and fore Trial, he will not forfake us though he chaften us. Yea, father (faid fhe) our heavenly Father doth Chaften us for our profit, that we may be partakers of his holinefs; no cha-ftifement feemeth for the prefent to be joyous, but grievous, but after-

wards it yieldeth the peaceable fruit
of righteousnels to them which are
exercifed thereby. The Lord is now
chaftening of me upon this fick bed,
but I hope he will blels it fo to me
as to caufe it to yield to me that
bleffed fruit, according to the riches
of his mercies which fail not.

7. After this fhe fpake to God
with her eyes lift up to Heaven,
faying, Be merciful to me, O Fa-
ther, be merciful to me a finner ac-
cording to thy word.

8. Then looking upon her for-
rowful Parents, fhe faid; It is faid,
*Caft thy burden upon the Lord, and
he fhall fuftain thee, and he will never
fuffer the righteous to be moved.*
Therefore, my dear father and mo-
ther, caft all your care upon him who
caufes all things to go well that do
concern you.

9. Her mother faid unto her, O
my dear child, I have no fmall com-
fort from the Lord in thee, and the
fruit of his grace whereby thou haft
been

been so much exercised unto godliness in reading the Word, in Prayer and gracious Discourse, to the edification of thy self and us. The Lord himself who gave thee to us, make up this loss, if it be his pleasure to take thee away from us.

10. Dear mother (said she) though I leave you and you me, yet God will never leave us; for it is said, *Can a woman forget her sucking Child, that she should not have compassion on the fruit of her womb, yet will not I forget thee, behold I have graven thee upon the palms of my hands.* O comfortable words both for mothers and children! Mark, dear Mother, how fast the Lord keeps and holdeth his people, that he doth even grave them upon the palms of his hands. Though I must part with you, and you with me, yet blessed be God, he will never part either from you or me.

11. Being weary with much speaking she desired to rest a while,

but

but after a little time awaking a-
gain, her father asked her how it
was with her? She made no direct
anfwer, but asked what day it was?
her father faid it was the Lords day.
Well then, faid fhe, have you given
up my name to be remembred in
the publick Prayers of the Church:
Her father told her he had. I have
learnt, faid fhe, that the effectual
fervent Prayer of the righteous avail-
eth much.

12. She had a very high efteem
for the faithful Minifters of Chrift,
and much defired their company
where fhe was; but knowing the
hazards that fuch a vifit might ex-
pofe them and the Church to, fhe
would by no means fuffer that the
Minifters fhould come near her per-
fon, but chofe rather to throw her
felf upon the armes of the Lord, and
to improve that knowledge fhe had
in the Word, and her former expe-
rience, and the vifits of private
Chriftians, and thofe which the
Church

Church had appointed in such caſes to viſit and comfort the ſick.

13. One of thoſe which came to viſit her, was of very great uſe to her to comfort her, and lift her up in ſome meaſure above the fears of death.

14. Though young, ſhe was very much concerned for the intereſt of God and Religion, for Goſpel Miniſters, and for the Sins and the Decay of the power of Godlineſs in her own Countrey; which will further appear by what may follow.

15. Her father coming in to her, found her in an extraordinary paſſion of weeping, and askt her what was the cauſe of her great ſorrow? She anſwered, have I not cauſe to weep, when I hear that *Domine de Wit* was taken ſick this day in his Pulpit; and went home very ill? Is not this a ſad ſign of Gods diſpleaſure to our Countrey, when God ſmiteth ſuch a faithful Paſtor.

16. She had a high valuation of
God,

God, and could speak in *David's*
language, *whom have I in Heaven
but thee, and there is none on earth
that I can desire in comparison of thee.*
She was much lifted up above the
fears of Death; what else was the
meaning of such expressions as these?
*O how do I long! even as the Heart
panteth after the water-brooks, so my
soul panteth after thee, O God, for God,
the living God, when shall I come and
appear before God.*

17. She was a great hater of sin,
and did with much grief and self-
abhorrency reflect upon it; but that
which lay most upon her heart was
the Corruption of her Nature and
Original Sin. How oft would she
cry out in the words of the Psalm-
ist, *Behold I was shapen in iniquity,
and in sin did my mother conceive me,
and I was altogether born in sin:* She
could never lay her self low enough
under a sense of that Original Sin
which she brought with her into
the world.

18. She

18. She spake many things very judiciously of the old man and putting it off, and of the new man and putting that on; which shewed that she was no stranger to conversion, and that she in some measure understood what Mortificacion, Self-denial and taking up of her Cross, and following of Christ meant. That Scripture was much in her mouth, *The sacrifices of God are a contrite heart; a broken and a contrite spirit, O God, thou wilt not despise.* That brokenness of heart (said she) which is built upon and flows from faith, and that faith which is built upon Christ, who is the proper and alone Sacrifice for Sin. These are her own words.

19. Afterwards she desired to rest, and when she had slumbred a while, she said, O dear father and Mother, how weak do I feel my self! My dear Child (said her father) God will in his tender mercy strengthen thee in thy weakness.

Yea

Yea father (said she) that is my confidence: For it is said, *The bruised reed he will not break, and the smoking flax he will not quench.*

20. Then she discoursed excellently of the nature of Faith, and desired that the eleventh of the *Hebrews* should be read unto her; at the reading of which she cryed out, O what a stedfast loyal faith was that of *Abraham*, which made him willing to offer up his own and only Son! Faith is the substance of things hoped for, the evidence of things not seen.

21. Her Father and Mother hearing her excellent discourse, and seeing her admirable carriage, burst out into abundance of tears: upon which she pleaded with them to be patient and content with the hand of God. O (said she) why do you weep at this rate over me, seeing, I hope you have no reason to question, but if the Lord take me out of this miserable world it shall be well

with

with me to all eternity. You ought
to be well satisfied, seeing it is said
*God is in heaven, and doth whatsoever
pleaseth him* : and do you not pray
every day, that the Will of God
may be done upon earth as it is in
heaven. Now farther this is Gods
will that I should lie upon this sick
bed, and of this disease; shall we
not be content when our Prayers
are answered? Would not your
extreme sorrow be murmuring a-
gainst God, without whose good
pleasure nothing comes to pass. Al-
though I am struck with this sad
disease, yet because it is the will of
God, that doth silence me, and I
will as long as I live pray that Gods
will may be done and not mine.

22. Seeing her Parents still very
much moved, she further argued
with them from the Providence of
God, which had a special hand in
every common thing, much more in
the disposal of the lives of men and
women: *Are not two Sparrows
sold*

fold for a farthing, and not one of
them falls to the ground without our
heavenly Father? Yea, *the hairs*
of our head are a'l numbred; there-
fore fear not, you are of more value
than many Sparrows. · Adverſity and
Proſperity they are both good. Some
things ſeem evil in our eyes, but
the Lord turns all to the good of them
which are his.

23. She came then to ſpeak par-
ticularly concerning the Plague,
Doth not (ſaid ſhe) the Peſtilence
come from God; why elſe doth
the Scripture ſay, *ſhall there be evil*
in the City which I have not ſent?
What do thoſe people mean, which
ſay the Peſtilence comes from the
Air? Is not the Lord the Creator
and Ruler of the Air, and are not
the Elements under his Govern-
ment? Or if they ſay it comes from
the Earth, hath he not the ſame
power and influence upon that too?
What talk they of a Ship that came
from *Africa*; have we not read long
ago

ago together out of *Lev.* 26. 25. *I shall bring a sword upon you, and avenge the quarrel of my covenant, and when you are assembled in the Cities, then will I bring the pestilence in the midst of you.*

24. After this, having taken some little rest, she said, O now is the day for the opening of the first question of the Catechism, and if we were there, we should hear, that whether in death or life a Believer is Christs, who hath redeemed us by his own precious blood from the power of the Devil; and then she quoted, *Rom.* 14. 7, 8. *For none of us liveth unto himself, and none of us dieth to himself. For whether we live we live unto the Lord, and whether we die we die unto the Lord, whether then we live or die, we are the Lords.* Then be comforted, for whether I live or die, I am the Lords. O why do you afflict your selves thus? but what shall I say? with weeping I came into the world, and with

weep-

weeping I muſt go out again. O my dear Parents, better is the day of my death than the day of my birth.

25. When ſhe had thus encouraged her Father and Mother, ſhe deſired her Father to pray with her, and to requeſt of the Lord that ſhe might have a quiet and peaceable paſſage into another world.

26. After her father had prayed for her, he asked her whether he ſhould ſend for the Phyſician; ſhe anſwered, by no means, for I am now beyond the help of Doctors. But ſaid he, my Child, we are to uſe the ordinary means appointed by the Lord for our help as long as we live, and let the Lord do as ſeemeth good in his eyes. But ſaid ſhe, give me the heavenly Phyſician he is the only helper, doth not he ſay, *Come unto me ye that are weary and heavy laden, and I will give ye reſt*, and doth not he bid us call upon him in the day of diſtreſs, and he will deliver us, and we ſhall glorifie him:

There-

Therefore, dear father, call upon him yet again for me.

27. About this time a Christian friend came in to visit her, who was not a little comforted when he heard and saw so much of the grace of God living in a poor young thing, which could not but so far affect him as to draw tears of joy and admiration from him, and her deportment was so teaching, that he could not but acknowledg himself greatly edifi'd and improv'd by her carriage and language.

28. That which was not the least observable in her, was the ardent affection she had for the holy Scriptures and her Catechism, in which she was throughly instructed by the godly Divines of the place where she lived which she could not but own as one of the greatest mercies next the Lord Christ. O how did she bless God for her Catechism, and beg of her Father to go particularly to those Ministers that had taken so much pains with her to instruct her in her Catechism, and to thank them from her a dying Child for their good in-

ſtructions, and to let them under-
ſtand, for their encouragement to
go on in that work of Catechiſing,
how refreſhing thoſe truths were
now to her in the hour of her di-
ſtreſs. O that ſweet catechiſing, ſaid
ſhe, unto which I did always reſort
with gladneſs, and attended without
wearineſs!

29. She was much above the
vanities of the world, and took no
pleaſure at all in thoſe things which
uſually take up the heart and time
of young ones. She would ſay, that
ſhe was grieved and aſhamed both
for young and old, to ſee how glad
and mad they were upon vanity.
and how fooliſhly they ſpent their
time.

30. She was not forgetful of the
care and love of her Maſter and
Miſtreſs which taught her to read
and work, but ſhe deſired that
thanks might alſo be particularly
given to them. Indeed ſhe thought
ſhe could never be thankful enough
both

both to God and man for that kindneſs that ſhe had experience of: But again and again ſhe deſired to be ſure to thank the Miniſters that inſtructed her either by catechiſing or preaching.

31. After ſome reſt her Father askt her again how ſhe did, and began to expreſs ſomewhat of that ſatisfaction and joy that he had taken in her former diligence in her reading the Scriptures and writing, and her dutifulneſs, and that great progreſs that ſhe had made in the things of God, upon which ſhe humbly and ſweetly deſired to own God and his kindeſs in her godly education, and ſaid that ſhe eſteemed her holy education under ſuch Parents and Miniſters as a greater portion than ten thouſand Gilders, for thereby I have learned to comfort my ſelf out of the Word of God, which the World beſides could never have afforded.

32. Her Father perceiving her to
grow

grow very weak, said, I perceive
Child thou art very weak: It is
true Sir (said she) I feel my weak-
nefs increafeth, and I fee your for-
row increafing too, which is a piece
of my affliction; be content, I pray
you, it is the Lord which doth it,
and let you and I fay with *David*,
*Let us fall into the Lords hands, for
his mercies are great.*

33. She laid a great charge upon
her Parents not to be over-grieved
for her after her death, urging that
of *David* upon them, while the
Child was fick, he fafted and wept,
but when it died, he wafhed his
face and fat up and eat, and faid,
*Can I bring him back again from
death, I fhall go to him but he fhall
not return to me.* So ought you to
fay after my death, our Child is
well, for we know it fhall be well
with them that truft in the Lord.
She did lay a more particular and
ftreight charge upon her mother;
faying to her, dear mother, who
have

have done so much for me, you must promise me one thing before I die; and that is, that you will not sorrow over-much for me: I speak thus to you, because I am afraid of your great affection; consider others Losses what they have been; Remember *Job*; forget not what Christ foretold; *In the world you shall have tribulation, but be of good cheer in me you shall have peace;* and must the Apostles suffer so great tribulation, and must we suffer none? Did not Jesus Christ my only Life and Saviour sweat drops of blood? Was he not in a bitter agony, mocked, spit at, nailed to the Cross, and a Spear thrust thorow his blessed side, and all this for my sake, for my stinking sins sake? did not he cry out, *my God, my God, why hast thou forsaken me?* Did not Christ hang naked upon the Cross to purchase for me the garments of salvation, and to cloth me with his righteousness, for there

C   is

is Salvation in no other name.

34. Being very feeble and weak, she said, O if I might quietly sleep in the bosome of Jesus ! and that till then he would strengthen me ! O that he would take me into his arms as he did those little ones, where he said, *Suffer little children to come unto me, for of such is the kingdom of heaven, and he took them into his arms, and laid his hands on them and blessed them.* I lie here as a child, O Lord I am thy Child, receive me into thy gracious arms. O Lord, grace ! grace ! and not justice, for if thou shouldest enter into judgment with me, I cannot stand, yea none living should be just in thy sight.

35. After this she cryed out, O how faint am I ! but fearing least she should dishearten her mother, she said, while there is life there is hope : If it should please the Lord to recover me, how careful would I be to please you in my work and learn;

learning, and whatsoever you should require of me.

36. After this the Lord did again send her strength, and she laboured to spend it all for Christ in the awakening, edifying and comforting of those that were about her; but her chiefest endeavour was to support her dear Parents from extraordinary sorrow, and to comfort them out of the Scriptures, telling them that she knew that *all things did work together for the good of them that did love God, even to those which are called according to his purpose; O God establish me with thy free Spirit! Who shall separate us from the love of Christ, I am perswaded that neither life nor death, nor angels, nor Principalities, nor powers, nor things present nor things to come, nor heighth nor depth, nor any other creature shall separate us from the love of God which is towards us in Christ Jesus our Lord. My sheep* (saith Christ) *bear my voice,*

2 G *and*

*and I know them and they follow me,
and I give unto them eternal life, and
they shall never perish, and no man
shall pluck them out of my hands.
My Father who gave them me is greater
than all, and none shall pull them out
of my Fathers hands.* Thus she
seemed to attain a holy confidence in
God, and an assurance of her state as
to another world.

37. When she had a little refreshed
her self with rest, she burst forth
with abundance of joy and glad-
ness of heart, with a holy triumph of
faith saying out, Death is swallow-
ed up of victory, *O death where is
thy sting? O grave where is thy victory?
the sting of death is sin, and the strength
of sin is the law, but thanks be to God
who hath given us the victory through
our Lord and Saviour Jesus Christ.*

38. That she might the better
support her friends, she still insisted
upon that which might take off
some of their burden, by urging the
necessity of death: *We are from the
earth,*

earth and to the earth we must return:
is the mother of us all, the dust shall
Dust turn to dust from whence it is, and
the Spirit to God which gave it.

39. Then She discoursed of the
shortness of mans life. O what is
the life of man! the days of man
upon the earth are as the grass and
the flowers of the field, so he flourish-
eth, the wind passeth over it and it
is no more, and his place knows him
no more.

40. She further urged the sin and
sorrow that did attend us in this
life, and the longer we live the
more we sin, now the Lord will
free me from that sin and sorrow.
We know not the thoughts of God,
yet we do know so much, that they
are mercy and peace, and to give an
expected end. But what shall I say,
my life shall not continue long, I
feel much weakness, O Lord look
upon me graciously, have pitie upon
my weak distressed heart. I am
oppressed, undertake for me, that

I may stand fast and overcome.

41. She was very frequent in
spiritual ejaculations, and it was no
small comfort to her, that the Lord
Christ did pray for her, and pro-
mise to send his spirit to comfort
her, It's said (said she) *I will pray*
the Father, and he shall give you
another comforter. O let not him
leave me! O Lord, continue with
me till my battel and work be fi-
nished.

42. She had very low and under-
valuing thoughts of her self and
her own reighteousness; what meant
she else to cry out in such language
as that, None but Christ! without
thee I can do nothing. Christ is the
true vine! O let me be a branch of
that vine! What poor worms are
we! O dear Father, how lame and
halting do we go in the wayes of
God and Salvation. We know but
in part, but when that which is
perfect is come, then that which is
imperfect shall be done away. O that

I

I had attained to that now: But what are we of our selves? not only weakness and nothingness, but wickedness. For all the thoughts and imaginations of mans heart are only evil, and that continually; we are by nature children of wrath, and are conceived and born in sin and unrighteousness. Oh! Oh! this wretched and vile thing Sin! but thanks be to God who hath redeemed me from it.

43. She comforted her self and her Father in that great Scripture *Rom.* 8. 15, 16, 17. *Ye have not received the spirit of bondage again to fear, but ye have received the spirit of adoption by which ye cry Abba, father. It is the spirit that witnesseth with our spirits, that we are the children of God; and if Children, then are we heirs, heirs of God, and joint-heirs with Christ.* You see thence father, that I shall be a fellow heir with Christ, who hath said, *In my fathers house are many* C 4 *man-*

mansions, if it were not so I would
have told you, I go to prepare a place
for you, and if I go to prepare a place
for you, I will come again and take
you to my self, that where I am there
ye may be also. O Lord take me to
thy self. Behold, dear Mother, he
hath prepared a place and dwelling
for me.

44. Yea, my dear child, said her
mother, he shall strengthen you
with his holy Spirit, untill he hath
fitted and prepared you fully for
that place which he hath prepared for
you.

45. Yea Mother, it is said in
the 84. Psalm, *How lovely are thy*
Tabernacles, O Lord of Hosts, my soul
doth thirst, and longeth for the Courts
of the Lord: One day in thy Courts
is better than a thousand; yea, I
had rather be a Door keeper in the
house of God than dwell in the tents
of the wicked. Read that Psalm,
dear Mother, therewith we may
comfort one another. As for me, I
am

am more and more spent, and draw near my laſt hour.

46. Then ſhe deſired to be pray'd with, and begged that the Lord would give her an eaſie paſſage.

47. After this, ſhe turned to her mother, and with much affection ſhe ſaid, Ah my dear and loving Mother; that which cometh from the heart doth ordinarily go to the heart, once more come and kiſs me before I leave you.

48. She was not a little concerned about the ſouls of the reſt of her relations, and did particularly charge it upon her father to do what he could poſſibly to bring them up in the ways of God. O let my ſiſter be trained up in the Scriptures and Catechiſing, as I have been.

49. I formerly wept for my Siſter, thinking that ſhe ſhould die before me, and now ſhe weepeth for me, and then ſhe kiſſed her weeping Siſter. Alſo ſhe took her young little Siſter in her arms, a

C 5 Child.

Child of six months old, and she
kissed it with much affection, as if
her very bowels had moved within
her, and spoke with many heart-
breaking words both to her Parents
and the children.

50. Her Father spake to one that
was by to take the poor little Child
away from her, from the hazard of
that fiery distemper, and bid his
daughter to give her from her, for
he had already too much to bear.
Well Father, said she, did not God
preserve the three Children in the
fiery furnace, and did not you teach
me that Scripture, *When thou passest
thorow the Fire, thou shalt not be burnt,
neither shall the flame kindle upon
thee.*

51. She had a very strong Faith
in the doctrine of the Resurrection,
and did greatly solace her Soul with
excellent Scriptures, which do
speak the happy state of Believers as
soon as their Souls are separated
from their Bodies, and what she
quoted

quoted out of the Scripture she did excellently and suitably apply to her own use, incomparably above the common reach of her sex and age. That in 1 *Cor.* 15. 42. was a great support to her, *The body is sown in corruption, but it shall be raised incorruptible, it is sown in dishonour, it shall be raised in glory; it is sown in weakness, but it shall be raised in power.* And then she sweetly applies it, and takes in this cordial. Behold thus it is, and thus it shall be with my poor mortal flesh, *Blessed are the dead which die in the Lord, because they rest from their labours, and their works do follow them. The righteous perish and no man layeth it to heart, and the upright are taken away, and no man regardeth it, that they are taken away from the evil to come, they shall enter into peace, they shall rest in their beds, every one who walked in their uprightness.* Behold now Father I shall rest and sleep in that Bedchamber.

52. Then

52. Then she quoted *Job* 19. 25, 26, 27. *I know that my Redeemer liveth, and that he sha'l stand at the latter end upon the earth, and though after my skin worms destroy this body, yet in my flesh shall I see God, whom I shall see for my self, and my eyes shall behold, and not another, though my reins be consumed within me.* Behold now Father, this very skin which you see, and this very flesh which you see, shall be raised up again; and these very eyes which now are so dim, shall on that day see and behold my dear and precious Redeemer; albeit the worms eat up my flesh, yet with these eyes shall I behold God, even I my self, and not another for me.

53. Then she quoted *Job.* 5. 28: *Marvel not at this, for the hour is coming in which all that are in their graves shall hear his voice and come forth, those who have done good unto the Resurrection of Life.* See Father I shall rise in that day, and then I
shall

ſhall behold my Redeemer; then
ſhall he ſay, *Come ye bleſſed of my
Father, inherit the Kingdom prepared
for you before the beginning of the
world.*

54. *Behold now I live, yet not I,
but Chriſt liveth in me; and the life
that I now live in the fleſh is by the
faith of the Son of God, who loved
me and gave himſelf for me. I am
ſaved, and that not of my ſelf, it is
the gift of God, not of works, that
no man ſhould boaſt.*

55. My dear Parents, now we
muſt ſhortly part, my ſpeech faileth
me, pray the Lord for a quiet cloſe to
my combat.

56. Her Parents replied, Ah our
dear child how ſad is that to us that
we muſt part *!* She anſwered, I go
to heaven, and there we ſhall find
one another again, I go to Jeſus
Chriſt.

57. Then ſhe comforted her ſelf
to think of her ſeeing her precious
brother and ſiſter again in glory.

I

I go to my brother *Jacob*, who did
so much cry and call upon God to
the last moment of his breath: And
to my little sister, who was but
three years old when she died:
who when we asked her whether
she would die; answered, yes, if
it be the Lords will. I will go to
my little Brother, if it be the Lords
will, or I will stay with my mo-
ther, if it be the Lords will. But
I know that I shall die and go to
heaven, and to God. O see, how
so small a babe had so much given
it to behave it self every way, and in
all things so submissively to the
will of God, as if it had no will
of its own; but if it be the will of
God, if it please God, nothing
for her, but what was the will and
pleasure of God: And therefore,
dear Father and Mother, give the
Lord thanks for this his free and
rich grace, and then I shall the more
gladly be gone. Be gracious then,
O Lord, unto me also, be gracious

to me. Wash me thorowly from my unrighteoufnefs, and cleanfe me from my fin.

58. After this her fpirit was refrefhed with the fenfe of the pardon of her Sins, which made her to cry out, Behold God hath wafhed away my fins, O how do I long to die! The Apoftle faid, *In this body we earneftly figh and groan, longing for our houfe which is in heaven, that we may be clothed therewith.* Now I alfo lie here fighing and longing for that dwelling which is above. In the laft Sermon which I heard, or ever fhall hear, I heard this in the New Church, which is matter of great comfort unto me.

59. Then fhe repeated feveral notable Scriptures which were quoted in that Sermon, afterward fhe defired to be pray'd with, and put petitions into their mouths, *viz* that all her fins might be forgiven, that fhe might have more abundant faith

faith, and the assurance of it; and the comfort of that assurance, and the continuation and strength of that comfort, according as her necessity should require. Afterwards she prayed her self and continued a pretty space.

60. When Prayer was ended, she called to her father and mother, and demanded of them whether she had at any time angred or grieved them, or done any thing that did not become her? and begged of them to forgive her.

61. They answered her, that if all children had carried themselves so to their Parents as she had done, there would be less grief and sorrow on all hands than there is; and if any such thing hath escaped thee, we would forgive it with all our hearts, you have done as became a good Child.

62. Her heart being quieted with her peace with God and her Parents, she began to dispose of her
                                    Books;

Books; particularly she intreated
her Mother to keep Mr. *De Wit's* Ca-
techise Lectures as long as she lived,
for her sake, and let my little Sister
have my other Book as my remem-
brance.

63. Then she said she felt her
breast exceedingly pained, by which
she knew that her end was very nigh.
Her father spake to her as he was
able, telling her the Lord would
be her strength in the hour of her ne-
cessity.

64. Yea (said she) *The Lord is
my Shepherd, although I pass through
the valley of the shadow of death, I
will not fear, for thou art with me,
thy rod and thy staff they comfort
me:* and it is said, *the sufferings
of this present life are not worthy to
be compared with the glory that shall
be revealed in us.* Shall I not suf-
fer and indure, seeing my glorious
Redeemer was pleased to suffer so
much for me. O how was he mock-
ed and crowned with thorns that
he

he might purchase a Crown of righteousness for us: . And that is the crown of which *Paul* spoke, when he said, *I have fought the good fight, I have finished my course, I have kept the faith, henceforth is laid up for me a crown of righteousness, which the Lord the righteous Judge shall give unto me in that day; and not only to me, but to all who love his appearing.*

65. *Ye are bought with a price therefore Glorifie God with your souls and bodies which are his.* Must I not then exalt and bless him while I have a being; who hath bought me, ye bought me with his blood? *Surely he hath born our griefs, and took our infirmities; and we esteemed him smitten and stricken of God: But he was wounded for our transgressions and bruised for our sin, the chastisement of our peace was upon him, and by his stripes are we healed, and the Lord laid upon him the iniquity of us all. Behold the Lamb of God*

God that taketh away the sins of the world: That Lamb is Jesus Christ who hath satisfied for my sins. So saith *Paul, Ye are washed, ye are sanctified, ye are justified in the name of our Lord Jesus, and through the spirit of our God.*

66. My end is now very near, now I shall put on white raiment and be clothed before the Lamb, that spotless Lamb, and with his spotless righteousness. Now are the angels making ready to carry my soul before the throne of God. *These are they who are come out of great tribulation, who have washed their robes, and made them white in the blood of the Lamb.*

67. She spoke this with a dying voice, but full of spirit and of the power of faith.

68. Her lively assurance she further uttred in the words of the Apostle. *We know that if this earthly house, if our tabernacle be dissolv'd, we have one which is built of God, which is eternal*

in

in the heavens; for in this we sigh for our house which is in heaven, that we may be clothed therewith.

69. There Father you see that my body is this Tabernacle which now shall be broken down; my Soul shall now part from it, and shall be taken up into the heavenly Paradise, into that heavenly *Jerusalem.* There shall I dwell and go no more out, but sit and sing, *Holy, holy, holy is the Lord God of hosts, the Lord of Sabbaths!* Her last words were these; O Lord God into thy hands I commit my spirit, O Lord be gratious, be merciful to me a poor sinner. — And here she fell asleep.

70. She died the first of *September,* 1664. Betwixt seven and eight in the evening, in the fourteenth year of her age; having obtained that which she so oft intreated of the Lord, a quiet and easie departure, and the end of her faith, the salvation of her soul.

Exam-

Example XII.

*Of the excellent carriage of a Child
upon his death bed when but seven
years old.*

Iacob Bicks, the Brother of Su-
fannah Bicks, was born in Leiden
in the year, 1657. and had religi-
ous education under his godly Pa-
rents, the which the Lord was plea-
fed to fanctifie to his Converfion,
and by it lay in excellent provifions
to live upon in an hour of diftrefs.

2. This fweet little Child was
vifited of the Lord of a very fore
Sicknefs upon the fixth of *Auguft*,
1664. three or four weeks before
his Sifter, of whofe life and death
we have given you fome account al-
ready: in his diftemper he was
for the moft part very fleepy and
droufie till near his death, but
when he did wake he was wont ftill
to fall a praying.

3. Once when his Parents had
prayed

prayed with him, they asked him
if they should once more send for
the Physician? No (said he) I will
have the Doctor no more; the
Lord will help me: I know he
will take me to himself, and then
he shall help all.

4. Ah my dear child, said his
Father, that grieveth my heart:
Well (said the Child) Father let us
pray, and the Lord shall be near for
my helper.

5. When his Parents had prayed
with him again, he said, come now
dear Father and Mother and kiss me,
I know that I shall die.

6. Farewell dear Father and Mo-
ther, Farewell dear sister, farewell all.
Now shall I go to heaven unto
God and Jesus Christ, and the
holy angels: Father, know you
not what is said by *Jeremiah*: *Blessed
is he who trusteth in the Lord*: now
I trust in him, and he will bless
me. And in 1 *John* 2. it is said,
*Little Children love not the world, for
the world passeth away.*   7. A-

7. Away then all that is in the world, away with all my pleasant things in the world: away with my Dagger for where I go there is nothing to do with Daggers and Swords; men shall not fight there but praise God. Away with all my books; there shall I know sufficiently, and be learned in all things of true wisdom without books.

8. His Father being touched to hear his child speak at this rate could not well tell what to say; but, my dear child, the Lord will be near thee and uphold thee.

9. Yea Father (said he) the Apostle *Peter* saith, *God resisteth the proud, but he giveth grace to the humble.* I shall humble my self under the mighty hand of God, and he shall help and lift me up:

10. O my dear child, said his Father, hast thou so strong a faith?

11. Yea, said the Child, God hath given me so strong a faith upon himself through Jesus Christ that

that the Devil himself shall flee from me, for it is said, *He who believeth in the Son hath everlasting life, and he hath overcome the wicked one.* Now I believe in Jesus Christ my Redeemer, and he will not leave or forsake me, but shall give unto me eternall life, and then I shall sing, *holy, holy, holy, is the Lord of Sabbath.*

12. Then with a short word of Prayer, Lord be merciful to me a poor sinner, he quietly breathed out his Soul, and sweetly slept in Jesus when he was about seven years old. He died *August* 8. 1664.

Hallelujah.

Example XIII.

Of one that began to look towards Heaven, when he was very young, with many eminent passages of his life, and his joyful death, when he was eleven years and three quarters old.

1. Ohn *Harvy* was born in *London*, in the year 1654. His Father was a Dutch Merchant, he was piously educated under his virtuous mother, and soon began to suck in divine things with no small delight.

2. The first thing very observable in him was, that when he was two years and eight months old, he could speak as well as other children do usually at five years old.

3. His Parents judging that he was then a little to young to send out to school, let him have his
liberty,

liberty to play a little about their yard, but instead of playing, he found out a school of his own accord hard by home, and went to the school-Mistriss, and intreated her to teach him to read, and so he went for some time to school without the knowledge of his Parents, and made a very strange progress in his learning, & was able to read distinctly before most Children are able to know their letters.

4. He was wont to ask many serious and weighty questions about matters which concerned his soul and Eternity.

5. His Mother being greatly troubled upon the death of one of his Uncles, this Child came to his Mother, and said; Mother, though my Uncle be dead, doth not the Scripture say, he must rise again; yea, and I must die, and so must every body, and it will not be long before Christ will come to judge the

world

world and then we shall see one
another again, I pray Mother do
not weep so much. This grave
Counsel he gave his Mother, when
he was not quite five years old,
by which her sorrow for her Bro-
ther was turned into admiration at
her Child, and she was made to sit
silent and quiet under that smarting
stroke.

9. After this, his Parents re-
moved to *Aberdeen* in *Scotland*,
and setled their Child under an
able and a painful School Master
there, whose custome was upon the
Lords day in the morning, to
examine his schollers concerning
the Sermons that they had heard
the former Lords day, and to add
some other questions which might
try the understanding and know-
ledge of his Schollers; the question
that was once proposed to his form
was, whether God had a mother?
none of all the Schollars could answer
it, till it came to *John Harvy*,

who

who being asked, whether God had
a Mother, answered no; as he
was God, he could not have a Mo-
ther, but as he was man, he had;
this was before he was quite six years
old. His Master was somewhat
amazed at the Childs answer, and
took the first opportunity to go
to his Mother, to thank her for
instructing her Son so well, but
she replyed, that he was never
taught that from her, but that he
understood it by reading, and his
own observation.

7. He was a Child that was
extraordinary inquisitive, and full
of good questions, and very careful
to observe and remember what he
heard.

8. He had a great hatred of
whatsoever he knew to be dis-
pleasing to God, and was so
greatly concerned for the honour
of God, that he would take on
bitterly, if that any gross sins were
committed before him. And he
had

had a deep sense of the worth of Souls, and was not a little grieved when he saw any one do that which he knew was dangerous to their Souls.

9. One day seeing one of his near Relations come into his Fathers House distemper'd with drink as he thought, he quickly went very seriously to him and wept over him, that he should so offend God, and hazard his Soul, and beg'd of him to spend his time better then in drinking and gaming, and this he did, without any instruction from his parents, but from an inward principle of grace, and love to God and souls as it is verily believed.

10. When he was at play with other Children, he would be often times putting in some word to keep them from naughty talk, or wicked actions, and if any did take the Lords name in vain, or do any thing that was not becoming of a good Child, they should soon hear of it

D 3　　　with

with a witnefs; nay once hearing
a boy fpeak very profanely, and
that after two or three admonitions,
he would not forbear nor go out of
his company neither, he was fo
tranfported with zeal, that he could
not forbear falling upon him to beat
him; but his Mother chiding of him
for it, he faid, that he could not
indure to hear the name of God fo a-
bufed by a wretched boy. This is ob-
ferved not to vindicate the act, but to
take notice of his zeal.

11. He was a Child that took
great delight in the Company of
good men, and efpecially, Mini-
fters and Schollers; and if he had
any leifure time, he would improve
it by vifiting of fuch, whofe dif-
courfe might make him wifer and
better; and when he was in their
fociety, to be fure, his talk was more
like a Chriftian and Scholler, then a
Child.

12. One day after School time
was over, he gave Mr. *Andrew*
Kant

Kant (one of the Ministers of *Aberdeen*) a visit, and asked him several solid questions, but the good man asked him some questions out of his Catechism: and finding him not so ready in the answers as he should have been, did a little reprove him, and told him, that he must be sure to get his Catechism perfectly by heart; the Child took the reproof very well, and went home and fell very hot upon his Catechism, and never left, till he got it by heart, and not only so, but he would be enquiring into the sense and meaning of it.

13. He was so greatly taken with his Catechism, that he was not content to learn it himself but he would be putting others upon learning their Catechism, especially, those that were nearest to him; he could not be satisfied, till he had perswaded his Mothers Maids to learn it, and when they were at work, he would be still following them with

D 4　　　some..

ome good question or other; so
that the Child seemed to be taken
up with the thoughts of his Soul
and Gods honour, and the good of
others Souls.

14. He was a conscientious
observer of the Lords day, spend-
ing all the time, either in secret
prayer, or reading the Scriptures,
and good books; Learning of his
Catechism, and learning of the Word
of God, and publick duties; and was
not only careful in the performance
of these duties himself, but was ready
to put all that he knew upon a strict
observation of the Lords day; and
was exceedingly grieved at the pro-
fanation of it; one Lords day a ser-
vant of his Fathers going out of the
house upon an extraordinary oc-
casion to fetch some Beer, he
took on so bitterly, that he could
scarce be pacified, because that
holy day was so abused (as he judged)
in his fathers house.

15. When he was betwixt six
and

and seven years old, it pleased
God to afflict him with sore eyes
which was no small exercise to
him, because it kept him from
School which he loved as well
as many boys do their play,
and that which was worse, he
was commanded by the Doctor
not to read any Book whatsoever, at home. But, O how
was this poor Child grieved, that
he might not have liberty to read
the holy Scriptures; and for all
their charge, he would get by
himself, and stand by the windows,
and read the Bible and good Books;
yea he was so greedy of reading the
Scripture, and took so much delight in it, that he would scarce
allow himself sometimes time to
dress himself for reading, the
Word of God was his great delight. Yea, though he hath been
beat for studying so much, yet
judging it Gods command that
he should give himself up to read

ing, he could not be beat off from it, till he was so bad, that he had like never to have recovered his sight more.

16. It was his practice to be much by himself in secret prayer, and he was careful to manage that work, so as that it might be as secret as possible it might be, but his frequency and constancy made it to be so easily observed, upon which, one time one having a great mind to know what this sweet babe prayed for, got into a place near him, and heard him very earnestly praying for the Church of God, desiring that the Kingdom of the Gospel might be spread over the whole world, and that the kingdom of grace might more and more come into the hearts of Gods people, and that the Kingdome of glory might be hastned. He was wont to conuue half an hour, sometimes an hour, upon his knees together.

17, He

17. He was much above the vanities that most Children are taken with, and was indeed too much a man to live long.

18. He was very humble and modest, and did by no means affect fineness in apparel, but hated any thing more than necessaries either in cloths or diet.

19. When he perceived either his Brother or Sister pleased with their new clothes, he would with a great deal of gravity reprove their folly, and when his reproof signified little, he would bewail their vanity.

20. Once he had a new suit brought from the Tailors, which when he looked on, he found some ribbons at the knees, at which he was grieved: asking his Mother, whether those things would keep him warm. No, Chi'd said his Mother; why then said he, do you suffer them to be put here, you are mistaken, if you think

such things please me; and I doubt some that are better then us, may want the money that this cost you to buy them bread.

21. He would intreat his Mother to have a care of gratifying a proud humour in his Brother and Sisters, he did tell them of the danger of pride, and how little reason they had to be proud of that which was their shame; for said he, if it had not been for sin we should have had no need of cleaths.

22. At kisure times, he would be talking to his School-fellows about the things of God, and urge the necessity of a holy Life; that text he much spoke on to them; *the Axe is laid to the root of the tree, and every tree that bringeth not forth good fruit, is hewn down and cast into the fire.* Every Mothers Child of us that doth not bring forth the fruit of good works, shall shortly be cut down with

with the axe of Gods wrath, and
caſt into the fire of Hell; and this
he ſpake like one that believed
and felt the power of what he
ſpake, and not with the leaſt vi-
ſibility of a childiſh levity of ſpi-
rit. This was, when he was be-
tween ſeven and eight years old,
and if he perceived any Children
unconcerned about their Souls, he
would be greatly troubled at it.

23. After this, his Parents re-
moved not far from *London*, where
he continued till that dreadful
year ſixty five; he was then ſent
to the latine School, where he ſoon
made a very conſiderable Pro-
greſs and was greatly beloved of
his Maſter; the School was his be-
loved place, and learning his re-
creation. He was never taught to
write, but took it of his own
ingenuity.

24. He was exceeding dutiful
to his Parents and never did in
the leaſt diſpute their command,
(except,

(except, when he thought they might cross the command of God) as in the forementioned business of reading the Scriptures when his eyes were so bad.

25. He was exceeding contented with any mean diet, and to be sure he would not touch a bit of any thing till he had begged Gods blessing upon it.

26. He would put his Brother and Sister upon their duties, and observe them whether they performed it or no, and when he saw any neglect, he would soon warn them; if he saw any of them take a spoon into their hands before they had craved a blessing, he said that is just like a hog indeed.

27. His Sister was afraid of the darkness, and would sometimes cry, upon this account; he told her, she must fear God more, and she need then be afraid of nothing.

28. He would humbly put his

near

near Relations upon their duty , and minding the concerns of their Souls and Eternity , with more ſeriouſneſs and life , and to have a care of doing that which was for the diſhonour of God and the hazard of the Soul.

29. He was of a compaſſionate and charitable diſpoſition , and very pitiful to the poor , or any that were in diſtreſs, but his greateſt pity was to poor Souls; and as well as he could, he would be putting Children, Play-fellows , ſervants, neighbours, upon minding their poor ſouls.

30. One notable inſtance of his true charity, I cannot omit. A certain Turk was by the providence of God caſt in the place where he lived , which this ſweet Child hearing of had a great pity to his Soul, and ſtudied how he might be any way inſtrumental to do it good , at laſt finding a man that underſtood the lan-

guage

guage of the Turk, he used means to get them together, which he at last procured; the first thing that he did, was to put his friend upon discoursing with the Turk about his principles, whether he acknowledged a Deity which the Turk owning; the next thing he inquired after, was, what he thought of the Lord Jesus Christ. At which the Turk was troubled and put off the discourse, and said, he was athirst and an hungry; which the Child being informed of, by the interpreter, immediately went to a Brew-house near at hand (his own house being far off) and did intreat the Master of the Brewhouse to give him some Beer for the Turk, and the argument he used was this; Sir, here is a poor stranger that is athirst, we know not where we may be cast before we dye; he went to another place and begged food for him; using the same ar-

gument

gument as before, but his friends
hearing of it, were angry with
him, but he told them he did it
for a poor stranger that was far
from home, and he did it that he
might think the better of the
Christians, and the Christian Reli-
gion.

31. He would have a savoury
word to say to every one that he
conversed with, to put them in
mind of the worth of Christ and
their Souls; and their nearness to
Eternity. Insomuch, that good
people took no small pleasure in
his company. The Taylor that
made his cloths, would keep them
the longer before he brought them
home, that he might have the
benefit of his spiritual and Chri-
stian society; and more frequent
visits.

32. He bewailed the miserable
condition of the generality of
man-kind, (when he was about
ten years old) that were utterly
estranged

estranged from God, though they
called him Father, yet they were
his Children only by Creation,
and not by any likeness they had to
God, or interest in him.

33. Thus he continued walking
in the ways of God, ingaged in
reading, praying, hearing the Word
of God, and spiritual discourse, dis-
covering thereby his serious thoughts
of Eternity.

34. He had an earnest desire,
if it might be the Lords good
pleasure, to give himself up to the
Lord in the work of the Ministry,
if he should live; and this out
of a dear love to Christ, and
Souls.

35. He was (next to the Bible)
most taken with reading of Re-
verend *Mr. Baxters* works, especi-
ally his *Saints Everlasting Rest*; and
truly, the thoughts of that Rest,
and Eternity; seemed to swallow
up all other thoughts, and he lived
in a constant preparation for it, and
look'd

looked more like one that was ripe
for glory, then an inhabitant of this
lower world.

36. When he was about eleven
years and three quarters old, his
Mothers house was visited with
the Plague; his eldest sister was
the first that was visited with this
distemper, and when they were
praying for her, he would sob and
weep bitterly

37. As soon as he perceived that
his Sister was dead, he said, the will
of the Lord be done. Blessed be the
Lord, dear Mother, said he, you
must do as *David* did, after the
Child was dead, h e went and re-
freshed himself, and quietly submit-
ted to the will of God.

38. The rest of the family held
well for about fourteen dayes, which
time he spent in religious duties and
preparing for his death; but still his
great Book was the *Saints Rest*;
which he read with exceeding curi-
osity, gathering many observations
out

out of it in writing for his own use.
He wrote several divine meditations
of his own, upon several Subjects,
but that which seemed most admirable, was a meditation upon the excellency of Christ; he was never
well now but when he was more
immediately ingaged in the service
of God.

39. At fourteen days end, he
was taken sick, at which he seemed very patient and cheerful; yet
sometimes he would say that his pain
was great.

40. His Mother looking upon
his Brother, shaked her head, at
which he asked, if his Brother were
marked; she answered, yes Child?
he asked again, whether he were
marked, she answered nothing;
well says he, I know I shall be
marked; I pray let me have *Mr.*
Baxters Book, that I may read a
little more of Eternity before I go
into it. His Mother told him that
he was not able to read; he said,
that

that he was; however then pray by me, and for me; His Mother answered, that she was so full of grief, that she could not pray now; but she desired to hear him pray his last prayer.

41. His Mother asked him, whether he were willing to die, and leave her, he answered yes, I am willing to leave you, and go to my heavenly Father. His Mother answered, Child, If thou hadst but an assurance of Gods love I should not be so much troubled.

42. He answered, and said to his Mother, I am assured, dear Mother, that my sins are forgiven, and that I shall go to Heaven, for said he, here stood an Angel by me, that told me, I should quickly be in glory.

43. At this, his Mother burst forth into tears, O Mother, said he, did you but know what joy I feel, you would not weep, but rejoyce. I tell you I am so full of comfort,
that

that I cant tell you how I am; O
Mother I shall presently have my
head in my Fathers bosome, and
shall be there, where the *Four and
Twenty Elders cast down their Crowns
and sing Hallelujah, Glory and Praise,
to him that sits upon the Throne: and
unto the Lamb for ever.*

44. Upon this, his speech began
to fail him, but his Soul seemed still
to be taken up with glory, and no-
thing now grieved him but the sor-
row that he saw his Mother to be in
for his death; a little to divert his
Mother, he asked her, what she had
to Supper, but presently in a kind
of divine Rapture, he cried out, O
what a sweet Supper have I making
ready for me in glory,

45. But seeing all this did rather
increase then allay his Mothers grief,
he was more troubled, and asked
her, what she meant, thus to offend
God; know you not, that it is the
hand of the Almighty. *Humble
your self under the mighty hand of
God,*

God, lay your felf in the duft, and kifs the rod of God, and let me fee you do it in token of your fubmiffion to the will of God, and bow before him. Upon which raifing up himfelf a little, he gave a lowly bow, and fpake no more: but went chearfully and triumphingly to Reft, in the bofome of Jefus.

Hallelujah.

FINIS.

These BOOKS of the
same Author, Mr. *James
Janeway*, are Printed and
Sold by *Dorman Newman.*

HEaven upon Earth, or the best
Friend in the worst of times;
The third Edition Enlarged, Price
2 *s.* 6 *d.*

Death Unstung, a Sermon preacht
at the Funeral of *Thomas Mowsley*
an *Apothecary.* With a brief Narrative of his Life and Death, also
the manner of Gods dealings with
Him, before and after his Conversion: Drawn up by his own hand,
price 1 *s.*

A Sermon preached at the Funeral of *Thomas Savage*, Price 4 *d.*
A Token for Children, first and
second part, the price of each 6 *d.*

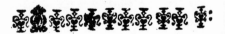

Preface to

The Holy Bible in Verse
The History of the Holy Jesus
The School of Good Manners
The Prodigal Daughter

The Puritans' acceptance of the doctrine of original sin compelled them to regard their children as reprobates. In *The Well-Ordered Family* (Boston 1712), Benjamin Wadsworth condemned children as "sharers in the guilt of Adam's first sin." "Their Hearts naturally, are a meer nest, root, fountain of sin, and wickedness; an *evil Treasure* from whence proceed evil things, viz. *Evil Thoughts, Murders, Adulteries &*." "Indeed," he concluded, "they're *children of wrath by nature*, liable to Eternal Vengeance, the Unquencheable Flames of Hell." Every child's natural tendency was to sin, the

PREFACE

Puritans believed. This is the view expressed in the following lines by the seventeenth-century poet Anne Bradstreet:

> Stained from birth with *Adams* sinfull fact,
> Thence I began to sin as soon as act:
> A perverse will, a love to what's forbid,
> A Serpents sting in pleasing face lay hid;
> A lying tongue as soon as it could speak,
> And fifth Commandment do daily break.[1]

Children were servants of the devil by nature; in order to be made into servants of God, their "wilfullness" had to be "beaten" and "broken" (to use the revealing words of the Puritan divine John Robinson) and their ignorance enlightened. To spoil a child was to appease the devil.

This is the underlying theme of *The Prodigal Daughter*, first published circa 1737-1741. The girl in this macabre tale is nearly ruined by her parents' intemperate love. Indulged rather than disciplined, untutored in the scriptures ("of the holy scriptures she made a game"), she grows up haughty and irreverent. The daughter's sin is disobedience; the parents', idolatry. The story thus affirms the Puritans' belief that their success as disciplinarians depended upon their maintaining a "due distance" between themselves and their offspring. As Thomas Cobbett warned in 1656, "fondness and familiarity breeds and causeth contempt and irreverence in children."[2] The disciplined child, the Puritans believed, was more susceptible to conversion than the spoiled child. "Restraining Grace is but common Grace," Thomas Hooker counseled, "yet by this means the work of conversion is more easie."[3]

Certainly parents bore a grave responsibility on account of original sin. As Dod and Cleaver pointed out in *Household Government*,

The young child which lieth in the cradle is both wayward and full of affections; and though his body be but small, yet he hath a great heart, and is altogether inclined to evil. . . . If this sparkle be suffered to increase, it will rage over and burn down the whole house. . . . Therefore parents must be wary and circumspect . . . they must correct and sharply reprove their children for saying or doing ill.[4]

The parents of the Prodigal Daughter are clearly culpable. Their love for their daughter prevents them from giving her the discipline that her depraved nature requires. The problem of loving too much, as the historian Edmund Morgan has suggested, was a very real one for the Puritans. It was probably because "they were afraid of spoiling them [their children] by too great affection," Morgan says, that Puritan parents resorted to the practice of "putting children out" to early apprenticeship.[5] *The Prodigal Daughter* is as much a warning to lenient parents as to disobedient children; it shows what may happen to any child loved "so dear."

Puritan parents aimed to maintain a "due distance" between themselves and their children not only for their children's sake but for their own as well. As John Cotton cautioned in 1656, "When we exceedingly delight our selves in Husbands, or Wives, or

Children," it "much benumbs and dims the light of the spirit."[6] To take an "excessive delight" in one's child was to love a wretched sinner more than God. Children should be loved, not idolized. Michael Wigglesworth put in proper perspective (from the Puritan viewpoint) the bond uniting parent and child in *The Day of Doom*, a fearful portrayal of the Judgment scene published in 1662. He depicted the Saints as listening unmoved as the sentence of condemnation is passed on those whom they have loved; even "The tender mother will own no other / of all her numerous brood, / But such as stand at Christ's right hand, / acquitted through his blood." The bond uniting parent and child was a *mortal* bond, a bond that death would dissolve. Increase Mather affirmed this view in 1711 when he speculated about

What a dismal thing it will be when a Child shall see his Father at the right Hand of Christ in the day of Judgment, but himself at His left Hand: And when his Father shall joyn with Christ in passing a Sentence of Eternal Death upon him, saying, Amen O Lord, thou art Righteous in thus

Judging: And when after the Judgment, children shall see their Father going with Christ to Heaven, but themselves going away into Everlasting Punishment![7]

Since only the Elect would be saved (and only God knew for certain who they were), no one was advised to grow overly fond of anyone else.

That he "was born not to live but to dy" was impressed upon the Puritan child from an early age. "Remember Death," Benjamin Wadsworth advised in "The Nature of Early Piety as it Respects God"; "think much of death; think how it will be on a death bed." Death was a recurring theme in Benjamin Harris's widely used *New England Primer*, as this verse on "The Uncertainty of Life" illustrates:

> I in the Burying Place may see
> Graves shorter there than I;
> From Death's Arrest no Age is free,
> Young children too may die;
> My God, may such an awful sight,
> Awakening be to me!

PREFACE

Oh! that by early Grace I might
    For Death prepared be.

"Young children too may die": this was the
unambiguous message of another widely
read children's book of the period, James
Janeway's *Token for Children*. The *Token*
offered "an exact account of the conversa-
tion, holy and exemplary lives, and joyful
deaths of several young children." Children
were not too little to die; nor were they too
little to go to Hell (in *The Day of Doom*
infants are allowed only "the easiest room in
Hell").

This being the case, parents were
obligated not only to discipline their
children, but to instruct them as well. "You
do an infinite *Harm* to your *children* if you
keep them in *Ignorance*," Cotton Mather
warned in *Cares About the Nurseries* (first
published in Boston in 1702). "This is very
sure, without *Knowledge* the *Soul* itself
cannot be Good. . . . Though every man be
not *Good* without *Knowledge*. An *Ignorant
Soul* will be a *Vicious one*." Parents should
teach their offspring so well "that it may be

said of them, as it was of a *well-Taught Youth*, 2 Tim. 3:15, *From a child thou hast known the Holy Scriptures, which are able to make thee wise unto salvation.*" *The Holy Bible in Verse* (first published in England in 1698 and in America in 1717) and the *History of the Holy Jesus* (first published in 1746 and frequently reprinted into the nineteenth century) were clearly intended to assist parents in the fulfillment of this important duty. They are pieces of propaganda, designed to impose unquestioning acceptance of Puritan doctrine on the children who read them. Their purpose is not to entertain but to sow the seeds of conversion. They reflect the Puritans' belief that "we are changed and become good not by birth but by education" (in the words of Dod and Cleaver).

The author of *The Holy Bible in Verse*, Benjamin Harris, was also a bookseller, publisher, and journalist. Harris began his publishing career in 1673 by issuing Benjamin Keach's *War With the Devil* from his shop in London. From then until 1679 he published numerous religious books, including diatribes against the Catholics and Quakers. An ardent Anabaptist and Whig, Harris joined Titus Oates in 1679 in "exposing" the Popish Plot. The following year he spent several months in prison for publishing a seditious pamphlet written anonymously by Charles Blount (*Appeal from the Country to the City*). After his release, he resumed his propaganda against the papists. His response to the failure of Monmouth's Rebellion and the accession of James II was to publish *English Liberties*, of which 5,000 copies were seized by the authorities. To escape fines and further imprisonment, Harris decided to join his Whig friend John Dunton in New England (Old England having become an "uneasie . . . Place for honest men").

Harris arrived in Boston in 1686. During his eight years there, he managed to establish himself as a prominent publisher and bookseller. On 25 September 1690, he published *Publick Occurrences Both Foreign and Domestick*, the first newspaper printed in America (it was promptly suppressed by the governor and the council), and sometime shortly before 1690 he published the *New England Primer*, one of the most popular and influential books ever printed in America. Harris returned to London in 1695. His newspaper *The London Post* ceased publication in 1706 and the last edition of *The Protestant Tutor* (first brought out in 1679 and said to have inspired the *Primer*) was printed in 1716. The date of Harris's death, like that of his birth, is unknown.

It is almost certain that while in Boston Harris made the acquaintance of Eleazar Moody, compiler of *The School of Good Manners*. The two men had mutual friends in the Sewalls and the Mathers.[8] Like Harris, Moody excelled in more than one occupation; in addition to being a schoolmaster, he was well known as a scrivener. He was in Boston as late as 1706 and died in Dedham in 1720. Although *The School of Good Manners* is attributed to Moody, and it is probable that he adapted it for use in New England, this work has a much earlier origin. Its ultimate source, as R. W. G. Vail has shown, was a well-known French courtesy book, the *Civilité Puerilé*, published in 1564. After many editions (in both French and English), the *Civilité Puerilé* became *The School of Good Manners*, published in London in 1685 and attributed to J. Garretson; this is the book with which Moody was probably familiar.[9]

"Tis very pleasing to our Lord Jesus Christ," Cotton Mather observed in 1699, "that our children should be well formed with, and well informed in the rules of civility, and not be left a clownish, and sottish and Ill-bred sort of creatures. An unmannerly Brood is a Dishonour to Religion."[10] That Mather was espousing the typical Puritan view is attested to by the popularity of Moody's book (no fewer than thirty-four editions appeared between 1715 and 1846). The Puritan view was that "wilfull" children, such as the Prodigal Daughter, were children whose evil natures had not been curbed; they were consequently doomed to "bring Disgrace on their Parents, as well as Contempt on Themselves" (as Moody warns in his preface). Well-behaved children, by contrast, were children whose

evil natures had been curbed: their
obedience to their elders bespoke their
obedience to God. The rules set down in
Moody's *School of Good Manners* were thus
aimed at keeping wicked children from
"visible outbreakings of sin." The under-
lying assumption is that children have a
proclivity for wrong-doing, which can and
should be checked. The picture that emerges
of the parent-child relationship confirms
what has already been said: it is ideally
authoritarian, the parent dictating to the
child and remaining aloof from him.

For the Puritans, Edmund Morgan has
pointed out, "there was no question of
developing the child's personality, of
drawing out or nourishing any desirable
inherent qualities which he might possess,
for no child could by nature possess any
desirable qualities." The will had to be
broken and a knowledge of the moral
precepts and doctrines of Christianity
instilled ("Though Knowledge may be
without grace, yet there can be no grace
without knowledge," observed John Norton
in 1654).[11] Not until the nineteenth century

would children cease to be regarded as "sharers in the guilt of Adam's first sin"; not until then would they cease to be feared. No one who believed in original sin could have claimed, as Bronson Alcott did in 1835, that "Childhood hath saved me."[12] Childhood for the Puritans was the most wicked period in an individual's life, not the most innocent. To use Joseph Kett's phrase, they viewed it as "a condition to be worked off with all due speed." It is hardly surprising, then, that the books they gave their children had as their primary object the foreshortening of childhood.

Elizabeth Williams

ELIZABETH WILLIAMS is a graduate student in the History Department of Cornell University.

Notes

1. Anne Bradstreet, "Of the Four Ages of Man," *The Tenth Muse* (London 1650).

2. Thomas Cobbett, *A Fruitfull and Usefull Discourse touching the Honour due from Children to Parents and the Duty of Parents towards their Children* (London 1656).

3. Thomas Hooker, *The Application of Redemption* (London 1659).

4. John Dod and William Cleaver, *Household Government* (London 1614).

5. Edmund S. Morgan, *The Puritan Family. Religion and Domestic Relations in Seventeenth-Century New England*, rev. ed. (New York 1966).

6. John Cotton, *A Practical Commentary, or An Exposition with Observations, Reasons and Uses upon the First Epistle Generall of John* (London 1656).

7. Increase Mather, *An Earnest Exhortation to the Children of New England to Exalt the God of their Fathers* (Boston 1711).

8. Harris and Sewall were fellow passengers on a voyage to London in 1688, the same year that Sewall's son Samuel attended Moody's school. Harris published some of the Mathers' books, and

the Mathers and Sewalls were of course acquainted.

9. R. W. G. Vail, "Moody's *School of Good Manners*: A Study in American Etiquette," *Studies in the History of Culture* (Menasha, Wisconsin, 1942): 261-271.

10. Cotton Mather, *A Family Well-Ordered; or, An Essay to Render Parents and Children Happy in One Another* (Boston 1699).

11. John Norton, *The Orthodox Evangelist* (London 1654).

12. Odell Shepard, ed., *The Journals of Bronson Alcott* (Boston 1938), 55.

BENJAMIN HARRIS

Bibliography:

The Holy Bible in Verse. London 1698 (two issues); reprinted London 1701; [Boston: John Allen] 1717; [Boston] 1718; [Boston] 1724; London 1724; [Boston] 1729 (two issues); Newcastle upon Tyne: John White, circa 1720s; Boston 1751; Philadelphia 1754; &c. See Welch 452.1 (492.1).

HISTORY OF THE HOLY JESUS

Bibliography:

The History of the Holy Jesus. [Boston] 1745 (no copy known); third edition, 1746 (two issues); fourth edition, 1747; fifth edition, 1748 (two variants); sixth, 1749 (two variants); seventh, New-London 1754; eighth, Boston 1762; tenth, Boston 1764; eleventh, Boston 1766; eighth [sic], New-London 1766; fifteenth, Boston [1767?]; tenth [sic], New-London 1769; twenty-fourth, Boston 1771 (four printings); eleventh [sic], New-Haven 1771; twenty-fifth, Boston 1774; twenty-sixth, Boston 1779; Worcester 1786; Hudson [N.Y.] 1790 (no copy known); Middletown [Conn.] 1790 (no copy known); New York 1790 (no copy known); Boston 1792 (two versions); Hudson 1793; New York [1793?]; Boston 1794 (no copy known); Worcester 1794; Hudson 1795; Boston 1796; &c. See Welch 532.1 (586.1).

THE SCHOOL OF GOOD MANNERS

Bibliography and Source Material:

Seager, Francis. *The Schoole of Vertue, and Booke of Good Nourture for Chyldren and Youth to Learne Theyr Dutie By*. London 1557. (A versified manual of prayers and precepts.)

Fiston (or Phiston), William. *A.B.C. Or, The First Schoole of Good Manners*. London 1595. (A suppositious title of the lost first English edition based on the original French work published 1564 by Christopher Plantin.)

———. *The Schoole of Good Manners: Or, A New Schoole of Vertue. Teaching children and youth how they ought to behave themselves in all companies. Also the manner of serving and taking up a table: With divers godly prayers, &c.* Newly corrected and augmented. London 1609.

Garretson, John. *The School of Good Manners.* London 1685.

Moody, Eleazar. *The School of Good Manners.* New London [Conn.] and Boston 1715. Third edition, Boston 1724; fifth edition, New-London 1754; Boston 1772; Boston 1775; Portland [Maine] 1786; Hartford 1787; Boston 1790; seventeenth edition, Windsor [Vt.] 1793; Boston 1794 two printings); Troy [N.Y.] 1795; Dover [N.H.] 1799; &c. See Welch 794.1 (871.1).

THE PRODIGAL DAUGHTER

Bibliography:

First published in Boston about 1737-1741, *The Prodigal Daughter* was reprinted many times throughout the eighteenth century—primarily undated, and thus difficult to distinguish by way of a short-title catalogue. A detailed bibliographical study of various editions, examining kinds of type used and punctuation, is contained in d'Alte A. Welch, *Bibliography of American Children's Books Printed Prior to 1821* (Worcester 1963-1967, also 1972), item 965 (1068).

SELECTED REFERENCES:

Bates, Albert Carlos. *The History of the Holy Jesus. A list of editions.* Hartford: Privately printed, 1911.

Halsey, Rosalie. *Forgotten Books of the American Nursery.* Boston 1911.

Fleming, Sanford. *Children and Puritanism. The Place of Children in the Life and Thought of the New England Churches 1620-1847.* New Haven 1933.

Nichols, Charles L. *The Holy Bible in Verse.* Worcester: American Antiquarian Society, 1926.

Stone, Wilbur Macey. *The Holy Bible in Verse 1698.* Worcester: American Antiquarian Society, 1935.

Vail, R. W. G. "Moody's *School of Good Manners*: A Study in American Etiquette," *Studies in the History of Culture* (Menasha, Wisconsin, 1942): 261-271.

Kiefer, Monica. *American Children Through their Books 1700-1835.* Philadelphia 1948.

Sloane, William. *Children's Books in Eng-*

land and America in the Seventeenth Century. New York 1955.

Morgan, Edmund S. *The Puritan Family. Religion and Domestic Relations in Seventeenth-Century New England.* Revised edition. New York 1966.

Stannard, David. "Death and the Puritan Child," *American Quarterly* XXVI (December 1974): 456-476.

Beales, Ross W., Jr. "In Search of the Historical Child: Miniature Adulthood and Youth in Colonial New England," *American Quarterly* XXVII (October 1975): 379-398.

The Holy Bible in Verse

Bibliographical Note:

This facsimile has been made
from a copy at
The University of California
at Los Angeles
Special Collections

THE
HOLY
𝕭𝖎𝖇𝖑𝖊
In Verse.

1717.

Christian Reader,

Whoe'er thou art, or of what Persuasion soever, surely thou hast some secret Respect for every thing which savours of the Oracles of God. Lo, here thou hast a Smell of that Garden of Spices, would to God it might ravish thy Heart, so far as to drive thee every Morning to pluck a Flower there-from. *Christian,* read it with Gravity, and you'll find it an excellent Antidote against a weak Memory. That you may turn *Berean,* and run ofter to its sacred Original, is the Prayer of thine,

B. H.

Genesis.

THis book *contains a full relation*
Of God Almighty's wise Creation,
Who by his Power in fix Days
The Earth did frame and Heav'n raife
Now Paradice is planted and
Adam is made t' enjoy the land.
How God, becaufe he was alone,
Made him a *Help-meet* of his bone,
Who is deceiv'd O worft of all !
From whence deriv'd man's fhameful
But yet by *Heaven 'twas decreed (fall*
Jefus *fhould* pay for Man's *misdeed*
Cain murders *Abel,* and his Blood.
To *God* for veng'ance crys aloud,
By whom he's curfed, & muft live
Upon the Earth a Fugitive ;

At

The Holy Bible,

At which he cries out in despair,
My *Grief* is more than I can b'ar.
Mans Wickedness *grows very great*
For which a *Deluge God does threat,*
It comes, & in it all are drown'd,
Save only *Eight*, who mercy found
God's Covenant with *Noah*, and
How he replenisheth the Land.
Noah is drunk, and naked lies,
Which shameless *Ham* his *Son* espies
His Father's Nakedness discovers
Immediately unto his Brothers.,
Who with their Faces backwards came,
And with a Garment hid *the same.*
He's cursed & his Brother's blest,
Old *Noah* dyes, and goes to rest.
Babel they think to build so high,
That it might reach *the* azure Sky.
But God therein *no Pleasure* found
And did their Language then confound
Abra'm for *Sodom* doth interceed,
Five times with God, but cannot speed.
Angels of righteous *Lot* take care,
Who with *his Daughters* saved are.
                              His

Epitomiz'd in Verse.

His *Wife* looks back, & for the fact
A Pillar she is made of Salt.
Joseph is sold to *Egypt*, and (Land
By *Pharoah* he's made Lord o' th'
Isra'l goes down with's Family,
To see his Son, & there does dye:
Joseph grows Old, and also Dy'd,
Then *Isra'ls* Children multiply'd

Exodus.

So fast, that *Pharoah's* Heart soon fails
Yet gives Command to drown the Males
But *Moses* God preserves, that he
From bondage might all *Israel* free,
And *Pharoah's* Heart is harden'd so
That he'll not let the People go.
Then *Plagues from God in number* ten
Destroy'd a Multitude of Men.
The *Isra'lites* are freed at last,
And o'er the Red Sea safely past.
But *Pharoah* thinking to surround
Them, *He and's Company are drown'd*
The People murmur & transgress
Tho' God with *Manna* doth 'em bless.
The Holy Law is writ on Stone,
To guide us to the great three One.

The Holy Bible,

The Ceremonies in this Word,
Are Types of *Jesus Christ* our Lord
Leviticus.

This Book *contains Jehovahs Will*
To *love* what's good, & punish Ill
Because that men are *apt* to stray,
It tells 'em *how* their God t' obey.
God's Name blasphemed *is* by one
Whom all the *Congregation* stone.
The Levites are appointed, who
Must Preach the *Word* his flock
      Numbers.   (unto.

Moses the People numbreth so;
That every Tribe to War *must go*
The *Isra'lites* to murmuring take
Which doth *Jehovah* angry make.
Korah, Abiram, and proud *Dathan,*
Are *swallow'd* up for *Recantation* ;
With *Og* & *Sihon's* faithless King
The Isra'lites to ruin bring.
An Ass doth *Balaam* here detain,
From being by an *Angel* slain.
The Isra'lites are strong in might,
And with five *Median Monarchs fight.*

             They

Epitomiz'd in Verse.

They kill them all & have access
Unto the land of Blessedness.

Deuteronomy.

The Law of God repeated is,
That Men no more *may* do amiss.
Moses a Song of Mercy sings;
Unto Jehovah King of kings.
Then *Heavenly* Moses *meekly* dyes,
And in a Tomb *unknown* he lyes.

Joshua.

Next *Joshua* the Son of *Nun,*
Immediately supplies his room.
Who *does obtain* from *Heaven* high
Instructions of God's Majesty.
Then *Joshua* with Courage great,
O'er Jordans River passed strait,
The City Jericho, they all
Encompass till down *fell the wall.*
Next Israel doth lose the Day,
And *Achan* steals the Wedge *away*
Five Kings are Hang'd, the Sun stands
Till *Joshua* his *Foes* does kill, (still
And one and Thirty others slain,
'Fore *Israel* did in peace obtain,

Their

The Holy Bible,

Their Land, when quickly it drew nigh
In which bless'd *Joshua* did dye.
Judges.
But still the Isra'lites rebel,
Till heavy Judgments on 'em fell.
Ehud, thro' Policy of Word
Kills *Eglon* with a two-edg'd sword
And *Deborah* with *Barak* does
Deliver Isra'l from their Foes.
And Hebers Wife, whose Name was Jael
Thro' *Sisera's* Temple *drove a* Nail
Jeptha does make a Vow to God,
And offers up his *Daughters* Blood
Sampson is born, a Man of might,
And with a Lion he doth Fight.
He Marries, and a Riddle told,
For the *Philistines* to unfold,
He by fond *Dalilah* betray'd,
The Riddle also known is made.
Sampson to *Askelon* down goes,
And killeth thirty of his Foes
Three Hundred Foxes tail to tail
With fire do their corn assail,
He with an Ass's jaw-bone then
Killed compleat a thousand Men.

Epitomiz'd in Verse.

Sampson to Geza quick escapes,
And carries thence away tne gates:
The Philistines with's Wife devise
To take him & put out his eyes,
When with enticing words so fair
His strength departed with his hair.
And then the Nobles made him blind
That be i th' Prison house might grind.
Which cruel act he did repay,
For he three thousand more did slay.

Ruth.

Ruth tho' she was a Moabite
Yet constant is in doing right,
Serving the Lord who makes her life
Happy in being Boaz's Wife.

Samuel I. II.

Hannah does bear a Prophet, who
She dedicates the Lord unto.
But Eli's Sons they do transgress,
By acting grievous Wickedness,
'Cause Israel doth God forsake,
The Philistines the Ark do take,
Whereat old Eli and his Wife,
With Grief departed both this Life,

And

The Holy Bible,

And Saul thro' seeking Asses sped,
Far better by a crowned Head.

The Lord doth Samuel appoint
David the Son of Jesse t' anoint.
Goliah with a mighty Host,
Over the Isra'lites doth boast
But David with a Sling and Stone
Made great Goliah tumble down.
Saul envies David and his Will,
With fury seeks his Blood to spill.
Saul's hatred now comes on apace
And David's glory doth increase.
David hath power in the Cave
To slay K. Saul but doth him save
The Philistines obtain the Day,
And Saul and sons in battle slay.
   David a Lamentation
Doth make o'er Saul & Jonathan.

Epitomiz'd in Verse.

He's crowned king, & up he goes
To *Hebron* there to fight his foes,
The Philistines and Moabites,
He does subdue, & Syria smites
Before the Ark he dances, when
With shouts it *was* restor'd again,
Then *David* gets the victory
O'er *Hanun's* wretched villany:

On *Bathsheba* he casts his Eyes,
And she's to Lust a sacrifice:
And for to hide this sinful stain
Causes *Uriah* to be slain.
Whereat th'Almighty *Nathan* sent
In order that he might Repent.
To Royal *David's* born a Son
Of *Bathsheba*, nam'd *Solomon.*
And *Rabbah's* taken by him when
He tortureth the City's Men,

The Holy Bible,

And *Abfalom* doth *Amnon* kill,
For forcing *Tamar* 'gainſt her will
For which offence *Joab* does *bring*
The Murderer before the King,
Where all is huſht, yet *Abfalom*
Doth at his Father's kingdom aim
But as he hung in th'*Oak* by's Hair,
He killed was by *Joab*'s Spear.
The News was ſoon to *David* ſent
And bitterly he does Lament.
David the people numbreth ; and
The *Plague increaſeth in the* Land.
Kings I. II.

K. *David* dies, & leaves the *Throne*
Unto the Wiſe King *Solomon* ;
Who's very rich & *wealthy* grown
Moſt wiſely Judgment paſſes on

The

Epitomiz'd in Verse.

The *Harlot's*, & does soon discover
Who *of the living Child was Mother.*
He sent for Workmen from afar
The Temple of *the Lord* to rear.
Before nor after found was one,
That e'er so *wisely rul'd the Throne.*
Yet he neglects his God, O worst
Of all to idolize his Lust ;
He dies, and by his Father's laid,
And *Rehoboam* does succeed.
Ahaziah 'gainst God rebels,
And Elijah his Death foretels,
'He does consume by Fire then,
Two Captains with *a hundred Men*
Elijah up to Heaven is tak'n,
But here Elisha doth remain ;
At *whom* the *wicked* Children jeer
Who all by *Bears* devoured were,
Elisha many Wonders by
God's *Spirit* works & so doth die.
This Book in general doth tell
some Kings acts ill & *others* well.

Chronicles.

The Tribes which from old Adam came
are Numbred to immortal Fame

The Holy Bible,

And *David's acts recorded are,* (care
That misled men may take more
This *Book unto remembrance* brings
The state of Isra'ls Judah's kings
And how Manasses in despair,
Finds Mercy in a hearty Pray'r.

Ezra.

Syrus the *Persian* granteth leave
The *Jews* their *freedom shall* receive
He to his people doth próclaim
The *temple* of the Lord to frame.
But *yet they hindred are* who build
By wicked men with malice fill'd
Till by God's leave *they* do obtain
Their Church and *Common-wealth*

Nehemiah.   (again,

The News is brought to *Hanani,*
Of *Jerusalem's* Mísery ;
Which holy *Nehemiah* hears,
And prays to God *with many tears*
And quickly after he begins,
To rectify abusive sins.

Esther.

Ahashuerus Men doth send,
That *Vashti* may on him attend;

Epitomiz'd in Verse.

But she refuses to be seen,
And *Esther* thereupon's *made* Queen
A Plot's contriv'd against *the King*
Which *Mordecai* to *light* doth bring,
But *Haman* by the King's advanc'd
Who seeks revenge the *Jews* against
And for which act he does obtain,
The King's *Decree* to have 'em slain.

Yet *Mordecai* to *Esther* sues,
Who begs the king to *save* the *Jews*
At which proud *Haman's* base de-
Reversed is immediately (cree
And *Haman* hang'd, whilst *Mordecai*
Is cloathed in the King's array.

The Holy Bible,
Job

This *Book doth* patient *Job* set forth
In his religious Life and Worth
How Satan does thro'. Calumny
Endeavour him to vilify.
To *damn'd deceit* the Monster flies
And impudence doth him disguise
Among God's sons his *hellish Sway,*
Presents it self a certain Day,
Jehovah's all discerning sight,
Soon saw th' *Eternal Fiend* of night,
Knew all his Progress thro' this Globe,
And that his envy swell'd at *Job,*
Gave him Commission to molest,
And try to storm his *peaceful Breast,*
When quick he flew more swift thanWind
To perpetrate what he'd design'd,

His

Epitomiz'd in Verse.

His Cattle he doth take away,
And all his Children likewise slays,
But yet he can't obtain his Will,
For God by *Job* is blessed still;
The *Devil* tempts him yet once more,
By *smiting* him with boils *most sore*
And makes his wife (O *wickedly*)
To bid him Curse his God, & die
Whom he reproveth without sin,
Tho' she a foolish Wife had been.
His three Friends by appointment
Condole his misery & woe. (do
Job cursing then his day of Birth,
Hates life, *and longs to taste of death.*
But God, who did his patience try
With Blessings him doth magnify,
His cattle strangely doth increase,
And riches to him comes apace:
Ev'n Sons to him the Lord *doth rear*
And daughters three who beauties were.
For which *Job* blesseth God always
So dies, being old and full of days.

Psalms.

Here royal *David* doth rejoyce,
With Instruments as well as

The Holy Bible,

Harmoniously he chants the Praise
Of *Job* with various *Notes* & Lays
How God Almighty's Voice doth
The very *Wilderness to shake.* (make
[O blessed Chorister that sings
Eternally Jehovah's Hymns!]
This Book in gen'ral doth discover
God's Justice, mercy, favour, power
       Proverbs.

   The Proverbs of Wise *Solomon*
(Who was K. *David*'s only Son,
Before our eyes like Pearls appear
Exhorting us the Lord to fear.
He bids his Son with care avoid
The subtle cunning Harlot's *fraud*
Exhorts the sluggard to awake,
And with the *Ants* Provision *make*
Then *Precepts* lays before our eyes
That to our souls we may be *wise*
      Ecclesiastes.   (try

The Preacher here all things doth
And calls them worse than vanity.
He in an ample manner brings,
Both *times* and *seasons* for all things
                    For

Epitomiz'd in Verse.

For all that Man doth here inherit
Will only serve to vex his spirit.

He bids the *Youth rejoyce*, but know
To Judgment he must come also.
And in conclusion bids man to
Fear God and his Commandments do.
   Solomon's Song.
 This Love-sick Song of *Solomon's*
To Jesus and his Church belongs
And in this blessed Song we read
How *Christ and's Church* are married
O Lord unto thy Church and thee
Wedded my Soul desires to be.
This Song a Myst'ry is therefore,
Who *reads it let* him *Grace* implore.
   Isaiah.
Isaiah here doth Prophesie,
That Death & *Hell* shall conquer'd be,

The Holy Bible,

By Jesus Christ, whose Kingdom
A Sanctuary be to all   (shall
God's Woes herein *denounced* were,
'Gainst all things that *impious* are
The Godly will rewarded be
When sinners shall have misery.

Jeremiah.

This blessed Prophet prophesies
Of Jerusalem's Miseries,
For which the Clergy him *arraign*,
But *he in* Judgment's freed again,
Yet Jeremiah's beat and cast
In Prison, where he's shut up fast ;
From thence into a Dungeon he
Is thrown t' indure more misery ;
Till *Ebed Meleck* maketh Suit
Unto the King. and gets him out.
But now proud *Babilon* doth take
Their cities, and all captive make
King *Hezekiah's* Sons are slain,
And he himself a Pris'ners ta'en ;
Losing his Eyes & chained strong
To Babylon he's led along.
The rest contains in general,
How Babylon at last will fall.

Epitomiz'd in Verse.

Lamentations.

The Prophet Jeremiah here,
Wisheth his head a fountain were
That he might weep sufficiently,
For Jerusalem's Misery.
This *Book* may Exhortation bring
To all to have a care of sin;
Which did *provoke* the jealous God
To *scourge* them with a heavy rod.

Ezekiel.

Ezekiel is in Babilon
A Captive made, who calls upon
The Lord his God and Prophesies
Of Woes, and blest Felicities.
He many Visions hath, wherein
The Jews reproved are for sin.
By dry bones being made alive,
The hope of Israel does revive, (all
Christ's Kingdom promis'd, wherein
Upon the Lord their God will call
Israel o'er Gog obtains the Day,
And Princes are to Birds a Prey.
God's glory in the temple stays,
Whilst Priests therein do give him praise

Daniel

The Holy Bible,

Daniel.

This Prophet worſhips God be-
He Superſtition will adore ; (fore
Nebuchadnezzar dreameth, and
His meaning he doth underſtand,
Which to the King he does relate,
And for the ſame's *made very great.*
The King an Image makes *that all*
The people may before it fall :
But *Shadrech* with his *Brethren* two,
Nam d *Miſhach* and *Abednego* (turn
Before they would from Heaven
Reſolved in the Flames to burn.
And by the *Kings command all three*
Were flung therein immediately ;
But by the Power of Gods Arm,
They walk'd about & felt *ſo harm*
For which the King doth magnify
God's kingdom *in the Heavens high.*
He dreams again, and *Daniel* ſays,
That he in graſly fields ſhall graze
Daniel unto his God doth call,
T' unfold *the* writing on the wall ;
For which he by the *King is praiſd*
And thereupon to Honour raiv'd.

Epitomiz'd in Verse.

But yet he's flung by wicked Men
Into the roaring Lion's Den ;
But *Daniel* to his God doth call
Who sav'd him out of dangers all
But those mischievous evil Men
Were all devoured in the den.
Whilst King *Darius* makes decree
That *Daniels* God shall worshipt be,
The other Chapters do contain, (reign.
I think the time when Christ will
[Lord let thy Spirit o'er *me* spread
Whene'er this Mystery I read ;
But never let me in it pry,
Without thy blessed Majesty.]

Hosea.

The blessed Prophets Prophecy
'Gainst Whoredom and Idolatry ;
Briefly to Israel doth declare (are
God's Judgments truly righteous
Exhorts them with a good intent,
To leave off Sinning and Repent.

Joel.

And Joel tells the Jews withal
Immediate wrath *will* on 'em fall.
Without

The Holy Bible,

Without *repentance* which will be
A ſtop unto their miſery.

Amos.

The Iſralites are wanton grown,
At which *Jehovah* s brow *does frown*
And then God threatens Iſrael
That miſery ſhall with 'em dwell.
But by the Prophet *Amos* sPrayer,
Thoſe Judgments then diverted

Obadiah.   (were.

And now for *Edom's* ruin look
I th' Prophet Obadiah s Book:
For pride & wrong to Jacob they
Juſtly became bleſt Iſra ls prey.

Jonah.

Jonah to Nineveh is ſent,
But he to Joppa ſtraitways went,
And in a ſhip toards Tarſhiſh he
From *God Almighty* s face doth flee.
A ſtorm ariſeth and they all
Each to his God for help doth call
But all will not appeaſe the Sea;
Till ev ry one by Lotts agree
The evil Perſon for to tell ;
When lo, the Lott on *Jonah* fell,

Epitomiz'd in Verse.

Ionah they over-board do hale:
Where he's swallow'd by a Whale.

Three days and nights he doth remain,
Therein when he is freed again,
And then to Nineveh he went,
Where at his word they all repent
[If this thy Prophet must. O Lord
To do thy will be thereto spurr'd
What will become *of* stubborn *me,*
Who's ten times far more dull than
Spar me O Lord *but let me find* (he
As thou art just thou'rt *also* kind]
Mich 1.

In Micha's Prophecy we see
God's wrath against idolatry.
Princes are cruel Prophets all
To vanity and falshood fall,
The birth of Christ is prophecy'd
His kingdom conquest over pride

The Holy Bible,

Nahum.

The blessed Majesty of God
Unto his people's very good.
But full of just severities,
Against his sinful Enemies.
And God's *victorious* armies fights
With the rebellious Ninevites.

Habbakkuk.

The Lands full of Iniquity,
Which *makes the* Prophet *loudly cry.*
The whole in general contains
The Land is plagu'd by *Chaldeans.*
And *woes* thro' Sin denounced are,
Concluding *with the Prophets Prayer,*
Who doth therein submissively
Tremble before God's Majesty.

Zephaniah. (here

God's Judgments by the Prophet
'Gainst Judah still denounced are
Jerusalem's re prov'd, and then
It's restauration comes again.

Haggai.

The People by the Prophet are
Incouraged God's house to rear

And

Epitomiz'd in Verse.

And God that Man will keep from foes
Nam'd *Zerubbabel* whom he ha*in*
       Zachariah.   (chose.
The People are by Zachary,
Exhorted from their Sins to fly,
A Vision then is shown to him,
With Comforts for Jerusalem.
God of Jerusalem takes care :
And Zion's happiness draws near,
By Types good Zachariah here
Foretels Jerusalem's Welfare ;
Christ's coming to destroy *likewise*
All those that are her Enemies.
The Kingdom of his Majesty,
With Graces will adorned be.

Malachy.

Good *Malachy* doth here complain
That Israel's grown unkind again
The Priests by *him are sharply checkt*
Because their *Cov'nant* they neglect,
They irriligiously and vain
Offer polluted Bread Prophane ;
For which the Lord Jehovah high
Rebukes them with severity.

                     Th

The Holy Bible,

The People for Idolatry,
Reprov'd are by God's Majesty:
He sheweth that the Wicked will
With Judgments be attended still
And in God's Ire be burnt to Dust
Whilst ever blessed are the Just.
Then of *Elijah's* coming, and
His Office doth this Prophet end.

The *Apocripha*.

Th' *Apocripha* doth seem to carry,
A Sense from Scripture *quite contrary*
Which makes it thus by Church decree
From sacred Scripture placed be.
It tells how *Tobit* being blind,
Did by his Son Recov'ry find.
And how fam'd Isra'ls *Judith* did
Cut off proud Holifornes Head.
How that two Elders Lustful are
Who for Susannah lay a snare;
And tho' she keeps her Chastity,
Accus'd she's for Adultery;
But Daniel in the matter pries,
And finds the Judges Falsities,
Whereat Susannah Freedom hath
And both the Elders put to death

Epitomiz'd in Verse.

Next the deceit of th' Priests of *Bell*
Discover'd is by *Daniel.*
The *Maccabees* do most contain,
How many Jews in War are slain
How seven Brethren with their Mother,
All in one day the flames did smother.
And how for all the Tyrant's Threat,
These Martyrs did no Swines flesh eat.

The

The Author's *Caution to the* Reader.

THE Reader is hereby Cauti-on'd against a little spurious Book, Printed with the same Title as this, and shaped like it, as ignorantly and illiterately as can be, Printed by one *Bradford*, which Book is partly stolen from the O-riginal first Printed by *B. Harris*, Senior, partly Corrupted, and perverted in its Sense; and gene-rally the Word of God imposed upon with Nonsense, and Incon-sistency: so that the real Design of the Author is abused by such scandalous Imposition upon the Publick.

B. Harris, **Junior.**

March the 15*th.*
1712.

Epitomiz'd in Verse.

The New Testament.

St. Matthew.

LO from the Law, by Gospel he
Relates Christ's Genealogy;
How from old faithful Abram's Root.
By Joseph's Virgin Wife does sprout.
JESUS. God-Man conceived by
The Holy Ghost. for Sin to die.
The manner of whose Birth we find
Was on this wise to save Mankind
 Mary espous'd to Joseph just,
Was found with Child o' th' Holy Ghost,
Whereas this just Man tho't it fit
To use much secrecy in it.
His troubled Heart did Grief invoke
And inwardly his Mind thus broke,
The Rabble shan't with brutish Voice,
At her supposed Crime rejoyce;
But rather freely I'll agree,
Away to put her privily.
Thoughtful of this his Spirits fail
When careful sleep doth him assai'

The Holy Bible,

Fast in a Dream exempt *from fear*
An Angel thus invades his Ear,
Hearken to what from Heav'n I bring,
Joseph thou offspring of a King.
Let no fond fear disturb .hy Life,
But take thee *Mary* to thy Wife,
What tho' with Child she doth appear
Eternity it self lies there.
Her Chastity can safely boast,
It has conceiv'd the Holy Ghost.
And time with winged speed shall run,
Till her chaste Womb shall bear a Son,
A Son whom thou shalt *Jesu* name
That shall his own from *sin redeem*
Thus charm'd was *Joseph by the word*
Spoke by an Angel of the Lord,
When awful sleep his Opticks fled
The upright Man rever'd his Head
No *Doubts did harbour* in his breast,
Nor *how.* nor *why* his Soul possest,
But with eternal Faith supreme,
Did all that was commanded him,
Mary he took, & lov'd her more
Than ever he had done before

Jh

Epitomiz'd in Verse.

Yet knew her not till time proclaim'd
Her first born Son, whom Joseph
      (JESUS nam'd.
Wise Men from th' East directed are
To find Christ Jesus by a Star.
Joseph and Mary with their Son,
Into the Land of Egypt run.
Where *they do live till Herod's death*
When back they came to *Nazareth*
Then *John* repentance preaches and
Tells all God's Kingdom *is at hand*
Jesus doth come from Galilee
To Jordan, there of John to be
Baptized, when *God's* spirit bright
Like to a Dove on him doth light
When *God* the *Father* silence broke,
And from the lofty *Heav'ns* spoke.
Behold this spotless heav'nly One,
Is my own dear beloved Son ;
The Pleasures I from him receive,
None but a God like me *can* have
Christ fasteth in the Wilderness,
And by the Devil tempted is ;
He leaves him, & the Angels they,
In Ministration him obey.

The Holy Bible,

Jesus Repentance preacheth then,
To turn the Hearts of sinful Men,
Our Saviour *in the* mount *convey'd*
Open'd his sacred Lips and said,
Blessed are those made poor in Spirit ;
For they Heav'ns Kingdom shall inherit.
Blessed are they that Mourn and Weep,
For they at last shall comfort reap.
Bless'd are the Meek of humble Birth,
For they inherit shall the Earth.
Bless'd are all those whose chiefest Food
Is Righteousness to do them good :
Those Thirst and Hunger truly see,
Yet they at last shall filled be.
Bless'd are the poor in Heart, thro' Grace
They shall behold the Almighty's Face.
Bless'd are the Peaceable, who are
The Children of my Father dear.
Blessed are they who do partake,
Of Persecution for my sake ;
My Kingdom's theirs, & blest are those
Who bear Reproaches from their foes.
The Leper by Christ*'s touch is heal'd*
And by his word the Tempest*'s still'd*

The

Epitomiz'd in Verse.

The Devil by his Pow'r divine
From Men run in a *Herd of Swine*
Dead People by him Life do find
And Sight's restor'd *upon the Blind*
Christ his Apostles sends out, who
Have Power Miracles to do.
Those Cities he upbraideth then,
Where *his fam'd Miracles* have been
To weary Sinners, come, saith he,
For I your resting place will be.
John Baptist in a Prison laid,
By *Herod's* Oath *doth* lose his head.
Christ goeth to the Desart, where
Five thousand Souls to him repair
Who *all are with five loaves of Bread*
And Fishes two, by him there fed
Then walks upon the Sea *by Night*,
Which doth the Mariners affright
The manner of *Christ's coming* here
To judge the World, he sheweth clear.
And how transcendantly *there will*
Angels come down with Trumpets shrill
To make all from *the Graves arise*
And stand amidst *the Grand Assize.*

When

The Holy Bible,

When he from his eternal Throne
Juſtice ſhall execute upon
His Enemies. who then will ſtand
Like *damned Goats*, at his left Hand
The *Righteous* they will up aſcend,
To live where Joy ſhall never end
Whilſt Wicked with the Devils
In hell to all Eternity.　(Iye
Chriſt many Parables do ſhow,
Whereby we good from bad may know,
But yet his faithleſs Countrymen
Him and his Parables contemn.
He next doth many Miracles,
And *then his* painful death *foretells.*
Judas his Lord betrays to thoſe,
Who *are* their own ſalvations foes.
Before High-Prieſts he's led away,
And cloathed in a mock Array.
Peter three times his Lord denies,
With Oaths, with Curſes and with Cries.
And then Repents, but Judas he
Doth hang himſelf apon a Tree.
Jeſus i'th' Judgment Hall's abus'd
By *Jews* and barbarouſly miſus'd
　　　　　　　　　　But

Epitomiz'd in Verse.

But Pilate warned by his Wife
Is free to save our Saviour's Life
At which a multitude arose,
And *Barabas* the Murd'rer chose.
Who lifting up their Voices cry'd
Let him, let him be Crucify'd
Then Pilate taking Water, stands
Before them washing of his Hands
Freeing himself from it, when all
The wicked Jews aloud do Baul,
His Blood on us, & on our Children fall
Lo, then deliver'd up, he's script
With *mock'ry of his Robes, and whipt;*
And after they do him deride,
At *Golgotha* he's Crucify'd.
Nail'd to the Cross, his arms out-stretcht
Thro' Agony a Sigh he fetcht.
Whose voice all *thunders did out-do,*
Rending the Temple's Vail *in two*
Making the Earth *to shake, & those*
Who slept in Graves *forthwith arose*
And after he aloud had cry'd
Gave up the Ghost thus Crucify'd
Between two Thieves they do him rear
Piercing his Body with a Spear.

The Holy Bible,

And Soldiers thro' base Avarice,
Doth for his *seamless* Coat cast *Dice*
Bury'd he is by Joseph, who
The Tomb out of a Rock *did hew*
But by his pow'r in three Days,
His Body *from the Grave* doth raise
And in the mount of *Galilee*,
His own Disciples do him see.
He then commands them all to go
And preach his *word the world* unto

Mark.

Th' *Evangelist* doth here declare
John Baptists Office, what & where
Jesus Baptised is of John,
And casts a Devil out of one :
Cleanseth the Leper, and doth sit
Down with the Publicans to eat.
The twelve Apostles Christ doth chuse,
And who his Brethren *are* h e *shews*
By Parables he much doth teach
And of the Sower he doth preach,
And in a Ship he entreth then,
Expounding it to many Men.
The roaring *Wind* his Voice obeys,
And by his Word *the* Storm allays

Epitomiz'd in Verse.

Christ his *Apostles* now doth chuse
To preach his Gospel to the Jews,
And Gentiles, so that they may see
He came from sin to set them free
Among the *twelve Simon* by name,
Proclaims *abroad his* Saviours fame
The *fruitless Fig tree Christ* doth see
And cursed 'tis immediately.
The *force* of Faith he sheweth to
And how to Cæsar Tributes due
The Temple's lofty buildings he
Foretells will Ruinated be. And
False Christ's the Universe shall
And Wars & Famine plague Mankind.
Brother his Brother shall betray,
And *Children their own Parents* slay,
The *Sun and Moon* be darkned shall,
And all the Stars from Heaven fall
The Pow'rs thereof *will* shaken be,
And then the Son of *Man* they'll see
Come down in Cloulds by pow'rful m' he
With Majesty and Glory brig....
Therefore take heed, watch ye, and pray,
Since none there is which knows
(that day.

The Holy Bible,

Soon after this, the Jews agree
'Gainst Jesus by Conspiracy.
The rest, I think do most contain
How wickedly our Lord is slain ;
Likewise his Resurrection, and
How he to Heaven doth ascend.

Luke.

St. *Luke* tells how Elizabeth,
Of John the Baptist Conceiveth
And how from heaven Christ doth come,
To enter into *Mary*'s Womb.
John's Birth at *which* good *Zachariah*
Lifts up his praise to God on *high*
And at *our Saviour*'s Birth likewise
Old Father *Simeon* Prophecies ;
Depart, O let thy servant Lord,
In Peace according to thy Word.
Christ's *tempting Victory and Preaching*
Parables, Wonders, Meekness, teaching,
Disputing with the Doctors, and
How sick are healed by his Hand,
Are all related in this Book,
Of the Evangelist Saint *Luke.*

John

Epitomiz'd in Verse.

John.

John the Evangelist doth treat
Of Christ's Divinity most great.
In the beginning was the Word,
Which word was then with God the Lord
And *John* of him doth testify
His Office and Humanity.
The *Temple* by *Christ's* power divine
Is purg'd, and Water turn'd to Wine.
Shews the Samaritan his Zeal,
And *then the* Rulers Son doth heal
Philip Nathaniel findeth here,
And showeth *him his* Saviour dear
I am the Bread of Life, (saith he)
Who eats, shall live eternally.
Rebukes the boasting of the Jews,
And many Miracles he shews.
Christ *is the door, and Shepherd good*
And proves himself the Son of God.
He Lazarus to Life doth raise,
Who in the Grave had lain four Days
Mary anoints our Saviour's Feet,
With Oyntment, as he sat at Meat
A new Commandment Christ doth give
That we in Unity may live.

The Holy Bible;

To his Disciples he doth say,
I am the true and living way;
Therefore *let* Comfort you attend
For I the Holy Ghost will send.
Then prays to's Father heartily
To keep them all in Unity.
And then by Judas he's betray'd,
And to the Judgment-Hall is led.
Where they do mock and him deride,
And then with Thieves he's Crucify'd.

Acts.

In *Judas* room th' Apostles they
To chuse another did agree:
And as they pray the *Lord to know*
Which is his chosen of the two,
The Lot on Matthias doth fall,
Who numbred is among them all.
They being all with one accord
Together. praising of the Lord,
Were filled with the holy Ghost,
Upon the Day of Pentecost;
The Cloven Tongues of Fire fall
From high, & they're inspired all.
peter by Preaching doth Convert
Many from Sin and Satan's smart

Epitomiz'd in Verse.

Peter and John by heav'nly Pow'r,
From Lameness do a Man restore,
For Preaching in Christ's Name they
And of the same prohibited. (chi
False Ananias tells a Lye,
And falls down dead immediately,
His Wife Saphira doth likewise,
The Truth from Peter to disguise
But God in justice took away,
Her Life from her that very day.
On this great Fear did quickly fall
Upon the People great and small.
Then Peter many Signs did do,
Th' Omnipotence of Christ to show
The Apostle is in Prison cast,
Who by God's Angel is releast.
Stephen is Stoned, and doth cry,
Lord Jesus let my Spirit fly
To thee. The Eunuch strait believes,
And then Baptism he receives.
Saul in his persecution Road,
Converted's to the Son of God.
James killed is by Herod's Sword,
And Peter he is kept in ward.

But

The Holy Bible,

But he is freed an Angel by,
And worms *proud Herod doth destroy*
Lydia and the *Jaylor* do receive
Conversion, & in Christ believe;
Paul earnestly the Gospel then
Preaches to turn *the* Hearts of Men
He's put in prison, and the Jews
Maliciously do him accuse.
To Cæsar he appeals to whom
By Festus he is sent to Rome.
Which he at last doth safely see,
But not without Adversity.

Romans.

Paul to the *Romans* writeth and
Therein his Calling doth *commend*
Tells who justification hath;
None by the Law, *but* purely Faith
And who from Condemnation *free*
And how the Elect shall saved be.
With zeal their Souls he seems to move,
To'ards Faith, Hope, Charity and Love.
Advising with a good intention,
His Brethren to avoid Dissention.

Corinth.

Epitomiz'd in Verse.

Corinthians I. II.

Th' *Corinthians* are exhorted by
Th' Apostle *Paul* to Unity.
Christ Crucified he doth preach,
Not seeking Flourishes of Speech.
Of many things he doth them tell
In which they never can act well.
Paul the Corinthians fortifies,
'Gainst troubles and adversities.
His faithfulness in Ministry ;
And bids them flee idolatry. (tion
And *Precepts* lay for each Condi-
Exhorting all unto Contrition,
He glories in affliction, and
Wishes *their Faith may stedfast stand.*

Galatians.

Paul stands amaz'd at them to see
How *soon* they from the *Gospel* flee,
He asketh them the Reason why
From *Faith unto* the Law they fly ?
And *telleth* them when Jesus came
They *then were freed from* the same.
And in conclusion endeth thus,
It's best to glory in *Christ's* Cross.

Ephesians.

The Holy Bible,

Ephesians.

Herein he shews us *what* we were
By Nature, what by Grace we are.
Exhorts to Unity, and then
Saith angry be, but do not sin.

Philippians.

Paul prays to God for 'em. that they
In Grace increase may ev'ry Day ;
And bids 'em from false teachers fly,
And cloath'd be with Humility.
Then tells 'em all is *Dung & Loss,*
Unto Christ Jesus and his Cross.

Colossians.

Paul praises Jesus for their Faith,
And for increase in Grace he pray'th
That safely they to *heav'n may* go,
Their *Duties* he doth plainly show

Thessalonians.

They by St. *Paul* remembred are,
Both in thanksgiving & in pray'r,
Desiring them also to see.
To whom he sends young *Timothy*
And *how* we must for dead lament
And of *Christ's coming* to judgment.

Praying

Epitomiz'd in Verse.

Praying to God for them that *they*
May firm be in the truth alway.

Timothy I. II.

In these 2 Books we have at large,
How *Paul* to *Timothy* gives charge,
That pray'rs & thanks for all men must
Be made, & *Bishops* should be just.
And in the latter Days he saith,
That men depart shall from the faith.
Of his own death doth prophesie,
Then takes his leave of *Timothy*.

Titus.

In many things *Paul* him directs
How he must *deal with* Hereticks ;
The aged, young, & servants, he
Exhorteth to Sobriety.

Philemon.   (lemon,

Paul joys for the Faith of *Phi-*
nd begs him to receive his Son
nesimus, and saith that he
Nill satisfy, if ought there be.

D   Hebrew

The Holy Bible.

Hebrews.

The Jews admonished are here,
Their Saviour Jesus Christ to fear
And tells 'em the old Law is gone
Thro' Jesus Christ God's only

James.　　　　(Son

It is *not well* says *James* therefore,
To love the rich & hate the poor.

Peter I, II.

He them exhorts the Lord *to fear*
And says *the* judgment day *is* near.

John I, II, III.

Christ's *Person he describes,* & shows;
His death, & how from it he rose
Exhorts to persevere in Love,
Commending them to God above

Epitomiz'd in Verse.

Jude.

Jude does *the same* & says *they must*
Be punished who teach unjust.

Revelations,

Divine St. *John* revealeth when
The *Lord* of Life will come again;
How *gloriously* he'll *come* from high,
With power and great Majesty,
To judge us all. & burn up those,
Who are his disobedient foes.
He shews how *Antichrist* will be
Consumed by his Majesty.
And how for ever blessed shall
Those be who on his name do call

FINIS.

Questions and Answers out of the Holy Scriptures.

Q. WHo was the first Man?
  A. Adam.

Q. Who was the first Woman?
A. Eve.

Q. Of what did God make Man?

 A. God made Man of the Dust of the Earth.

Q. Of what did God make Woman?

 A. Of one of Man's Ribs.

Q. Where did *Adam* and *Eve* dwell?

 A. In Paradice.

Q. What cast *Adam* out of Paradice?

 A. Sin.

Q. Who

Quest. & Answ. out of

Q. Who was the best Man?

A. The Man *Christ Jesus.*

Q. Who slew his Brother?

A. *Cain*, because *Abel* his Brother was more righteous than himself.

Q. Who was the oldest Man?

A. *Methusalem.*

Q. Who was the Man God saved when he drowned *the* World?

A. *Noah.*

Q. Who wrestled with God?

A. *Jacob.*

Q. What was his Name called after he wrestled with God?

A. *Israel.*

Q. How many Sons had *Jacob?*

A. Twelve, of whom came the Twelve Tribes of Israel.

Q. What were their Names?

A. *Reuben, Simeon, Levi, Judah, Sachar, Zebulon, Joseph, Benjamin, Dan, Napthali, Gad,* and *Ashur.* These were the Twelve Patriarchs.

Q. Who

the Holy Scriptures.

Q. Who was the faithfulleſt Man that ever lived ?

A. Abraham, who is called the Father of the Faithful.

Q. Who was the meekeſt Man ?

A. Moſes.

Q. Who was the hard-hearted Man ?

A. Pharoah, King of *Egypt,* who was drowned with his Hoſt in the Red Sea.

Q. Who was the patienteſt Man ?

A. Job.

Q. What ſaid his fooliſh Wife ?

A. She bid him Curſe God, and Die.

Q. Who was the Man after God's own Heart ?

A. David, who was anointed inſtead of *Saul,* King of *Iſrael.*

Q. Who was the Wiſeſt Man ?

A. Solomon, who knew the Virtues of all Plants ; whoſe judg-

Quest. & Answ. out of
ment between two Harlots made
him renowned.

Q. Who was the strongest
Man?

A. Sampson, whose strength lay
in his Hair, when *Dalilah* his
treacherous Wife betray'd him
to the Philistines.

Q. Who wrote the Scrptures?

A. Holy Men of God inspired
by the Holy Ghost.

Q Who was the first Martyr
after Christ?

A. Stephen.

Q What Death did he die?

A. He was Stoned.

Q. Where was Christ born?

A. In *Bethlehem.*

Q Who was the Mother of our
Lord Jesus Christ?

A. The Virgin *Mary.*

Q. Who was the reputed Fa-
ther of our Lord Jesus Christ?

A. Joseph a Carpenter.

Q. Who

Q. Who betray'd his Lord and Master ?

A. Judas.

Q. What did he betray him for ?

A. For the Love of Money, which is the Root of all Evil.

Q. For how much Money did *Judas* Sell his Master ?

A. For Thirty Pieces of Silver.

Q. What became of *Judas*, after he had betrayed Christ ?

A. He went & hanged himself.

Q. Who denied Christ ?

A. Peter.

Q. What became of *Peter* after he denied Christ ?

A. He went out and wept bitterly.

Q. Who condemned Christ ?

A. The bloody Jews.

Q. Out of whom did Christ Cast Seven Devils ?

A. Mary Magdalen

Q. Who

Quest. & Answ. &c.

Q. Who are the best Children?

A. They that Fear God, and keep his Commandments.

Q. Where do they go when they dye?

A. To live happily with Jesus Christ in Heaven to all Eternity.

Q. Who are the worst Children?

A. They that Lie, and Swear, Steal, and break the Sabbath, and despise God's holy Commandments.

Q. What become of the Wicked when they dye?

A. They are cast into Hell, there to be tormented with the Devil and his Angels, for ever, and ever.

An

An Hymn.

'TIS not for us, and our proud hearts,
O mighty Lord, to chuse our Parts,
  But act well what thou giv'st ;
'Tis not in our weak Pow'r to make
One step o' th' Way we undertake,
  Unless thou us reliev'st.
When thou hast given thou canst take
And if thou wilt new gifts can make,
  All flows from thee alone ;
When thou didst give it, it was thine,
When thou retok'st it 'twas not mine ;
  Thy Will in all be done.
It might perhaps too pleasant prove ;
Too much attractive of thy Love ;
  So make me less love thee.
Some things there are thy scriptures say,
And reason proves that Heav'n & they
  Do seldom well agree.

Lord !

An Hymn.

Lord ! let me then fit calmly down,
And rest contented with my own ;
   That is, what thou allow'st.
Keep thou my mind serene and free
Often to think on Heav'n and thee
   And what thou there bestow'st.
There let me have my portion, Lord
There all my Losses be restor'd,
   No matter what falls here.
It's not enough that We shall sing,
And love for ever our blest King,
   Whose goodness brought us there ?
Great God, as thou art One: may we
With one another all agree,
   And in thy Praise conspire.
May Men and Angels joyn and sing
Eternal Hymns to thee their King,
   And make up all one Choir.

An Hymn.

MY God to thee our selves we owe,
   And to thy Bounty all we have,
Behold to thee our Praises bow,
   And humbly thy Acceptance crave.

An Hymn.

If we are happy in a Friend,
That very Friend 'tis thou bestow'st,
His Pow'r, his Will to help our end,
Is just so much as thou allow'st.
If we enjoy a free Estate,
Our only Title is from thee.
Thou mad'st our lot to bear that Rate
Which else an empty blank would be.
If we have health, harmonious ground,
Which gives the Musick to the rest,
It is by theé our Air is found,
Our Food secur'd, our Physick blest.
If we have hope one day to view
The glories of thy blissful Face,
Each drop of that refreshing dew
Must purely fall from thy free Grace.
Thus then to thee our praises bow,
And humbly thy Acceptance crave;
Since 'tis to thee our selves we owe,
And to thy bounty all we have.
Glory to thee great God alone,
Three Persons in one Deity.
As it has been for Ages gone,
May now and still for ever be.

A Prayer for King GEORGE,
for Success over his Enemies.

O God, the Fountain of all
Goodness, in whose Hands
are all the ends of the Earth, who
disposest of all Affairs as seemest
best to thy boundless Wisdom;
Lord stretch forth thy right Hand
and make bare thine Arm to de-
fend & protect *George* thy Servant,
& our dread Sovereign, from the
Power and Malice of those that
rise up against Him; Let their
Devices be confounded, & bro't
to nought that seek his hurt:
Let His Enemies be scattered
before Him, and Establish His
Throne in the Hearts of thy Peo-
ple, that He may be a true defen-
der of thy holy Church; that
Truth, Religion and Piety may
flourish and abound amongst us:
shower on Him the Blessings of
the Right-hand, and of the Left,
and

and glad His Heart with the
Melody of Joy and Triumph;
let His Reign be long and Happy
over us, and make us a willing &
obedient People, that so thy Favours may descend like the dew
of Heaven, on our Heads and
Hearts; and this we most humbly beg for the sake of Jesus Christ
our Lord. *Amen.*

A Prayer for the Royal Family.

ALmighty God, the Fountain
of all goodness, we humbly
beseech thee to bless His Royal
Highness *George* Prince of *Wales*,
the Princess and their Issue, and
all the Royal Family: Endue
them with thy holy Spirit, enrich
them with thy heavenly Grace;
prosper them with all happiness,
and bring them to thine everlasting Kingdom, through Jesus
Christ, our Lord. *Amen.*

FINIS.

The History
of the
Holy Jesus

Bibliographical Note:

This facsimile has been made
from a copy in
The Essex Institute
Salem, Massachusetts

THE
HISTORY
OF THE
HOLY *JESUS.*

CONTAINING

A brief and plain Account of his Birth,
Life, Death, Resurrection and Ascension
into Heaven; and his coming again at
the great and last Day of Judgment.

Being a pleasant and profitable Companion
for Children; compos'd on Purpose for
their Use.

By a Lover of their precious Souls.

The Third Edition.

Boston, Printed for B. Gray, on the
North Side of the Market. 1746.

Adam and *Eve.*

The Introduction.

THE great eternal God, who made
    The World and all therein,
Made Man also upright and just,
    And wholly free from Sin.

A pleasant Paradise the Lord
    Prepar'd wish beauteous Trees,
And all the Fruits thereof to Man,
    To eat whene'er he pleas'd ;

But one, and only one, and sure
    That could not be tho't much ;
But so it was, on Pain of Death,
    That Tree they might not touch.

For in the Day he eat thereof,
    God said that he should die,
And yet when Satan tempted him
    He eat immediately.

And

And thus he broke his Lord's Commands,
   And Death did thence ensue,
And thus Death comes, my Children dear,
   On every one of you.

And down to Hell you all had gone,
   Had not sweet Jesus flown,
To save the poor rebellious Wretch,
   From his deserved Ruin.

God having of his sov'reign Grace,
   Determin'd to save some,
In Fulness of his chosen Time,
   Sent forth his own dear Son.

And how he came, and what he's done
   The following Lines rehearse ;
O therefore diligently read,
   And ponder every Verse.

The HISTORY.

FOur thousand Years having roll'd away
   Now since the World began,
The glorious Son of God came down,
   To save his Creature Man.   The

The glorious blessed Time being come,
  The Father had decreed,
Jesus of *Mary* then was born,
  And in a Manger laid.

According to the moral Law,
  In eight Days Time he came,
And circumcised was he then,
  And Jesus was his Name.

The wise Men from the East do come,
  Led by a shining Star,
And offer to the new-born King,
  Frankincense, Go'd, and Myrrh.

Which *Herod* hears, and wrathful grows,
  And now by Heav'n's Decree,
Joseph with *Mary* and her Son,
  Do into *Ægypt* flee.

The bloody Wretch, enrag'd to think,
  Christ's Death he could not gain,
Commands that Infants all about
  Bethlehem should be slain.

But

Wife Men come from the Eaſt, &c.

Herod flaying the innocent Children.

But O to hear the awful Cries
  Of Mother's in Distress,
And *Rachel* mourn for her First-born
  Snatch'd from her tender Breast.

But soon the Monster *Herod* dies,
  And *Archelaus* doth reign,
When *Jesus*, our most blessed Lord,
  To *Nazareth* he came.

From whence unto *Jerusalem*,
  His Parents do repair,
To keep the Paschal Feast, which was
  Their Custom once a Year.

He then into the Temple goes
  Where many Learn'd and Wise
Great Doctors were, and doth dispute
  With them to their Surprise.

Our lovely Lord b'ing entred now
  Upon his thirtieth Year,
From *Galilee* to *Jordan* came,
  And *John* baptiz'd him there.

Now

Now as he from the Waters came,
 He lifts his Soul in Prayer,
And gloriously the Holy Ghost
 From Heaven doth appear.

In Shape like to a harmless Dove,
 The Spirit doth come down,
And Christ th' eternal Son of God,
 His Father now doth own.

He owns him now from Heaven above,
 And to the Earth doth tell,
That this was his beloved Son,
 In whom he's pleased well.

Now with the Holy Ghost being fill'd,
 From *Jordan* makes Recess,
And by the Spirit is led forth
 Into the Wilderness.

Where forty Days and forty Nights,
 He kept a solemn Fast,
And there the Devil tempts him sore,
 But Christ o'ercomes at last;

And

And after this our Lord returns
    Again to *Galilee*,
In *Cana*, where a Wedding was
    That Evening for to be.

Where by his great almighty Pow'r
    Both fov'reign and divine,
He, there to fhew his Glory forth,
    Turn'd Water into Wine.

Unto *Jerufalem* the Lord
    At the Paffover came,
And thofe that in the Temple bought
    And fold, he out did turn.

And many wondrous Works he wro't,
    When at the Pafchal Feaft ;
Where many were convinc'd, that he
    Was Jefus the High Prieft.

Then *Nicodemus* own'd the Lord,
    Acknowledging his Right ;
But lo ! thro' Fear of finful Men
    He comes to him by Night.

To

To whom our blessed Lord declar'd,
   Upon his sacred Word,
Unless that he was born again,
   He could not see the Lord.

And now to Christ the News was bro't
   Of *John's* Imprisonment,
By the ungrateful Multitude,
   His Progress to prevent.

From thence to *Galilee* he goes,
   Where he arriv'd at Noon ;
And after a retir'd Walk,
   To *Joseph's* Well he came.

Upon the Side thereof he sat,
   And lo a Woman came,
To draw some Water for her Flocks,
   Who knew not *Jesu's* Fame.

But Oh ! a happy Time it was,
   E'er all her Work was done,
She found the bless'd Messiah, whom
   The Prophets said should come.

Again,

Again, a noble Man of Fame,
   Hearing of Chrift the Lord,
Befought him earneftly that he
   Would Help to him afford ;

For that his Son was almoft dead,
   A Son to him moft dear,
When lo the Lord an Anfwer gave,
   Unto his earneft Prayer.

For the fame Hour of the Day
   That Jefus fpake the Word,
The Fever left him, and behold
   To Health he was reftor'd.

And now the Lord no Reft could find,
   From thofe of *Nazareth*,
To *Capernaum* therefore haftes,
   To find a fafer Birth.

Where from the Shore he launched out,
   And from the Ship doth preach,
The better to accommodate
   The Thoufands held to teach.

                When

When having clos'd ; launch out said he,
　To *Peter*, who obey'd,
And for a Draught immediately,
　The Net it down was laid.

Which presently was filled so,
　The like had never been,
For all the Men on board the Ship
　Were call'd to draw it in.

And thus unwearied did our Lord,
　Go round from Place to Place,　　De-

Declaring to a sinful World,
His free abundant Grace.

B   Aw

Away to *Galilee* he goes,
  In Synagogue doth teach,
Both working mighty Miracles,
  And wondroufly doth preach.

Unto *Jerufalem* again
  He comes at the Feaft Time,
And heal'd a Man that was difeas'd
  For thirty eight Years Time.

And there apologizes with
  The Jews that would him flay,
Becaufe that God his Father was,
  He openly did fay.

And from among the Multitude
  Of his Difciples there,
He Twelve did chufe and fent them forth
  To preach, to heal and cure.

Sweet Parables he alfo fpake,
  To name but one or two,
The poor, the loft, the prodigal Son,
  Speaks Comfort unto you ;

Wh

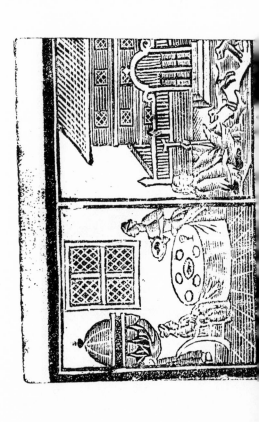

Who from your God have gone astray,
    By the Apostacy,
And if you will but now return
    Most welcome shall shall you be.

Another to reprove the Rich,
    And great ones here below,
To tell them of the fatal Doom,
    They'l have in Hell below.

Who when poor *Lazarus*'s at their Gates,
    Sit mourning, sick, and poor,
Will not so much as give the Crumbs
    That fall upon the Floor.

And now behold our Jesus works
    A Miracle indeed,
When at one Time five thousand Men
    He plent'ously doth feed,

With Barley Loves, no more than five,
    Two fishes, and but small,
And lo, refresh'd was every one,
    No Lack was there at all.

                        And

And now a King they fain would have
  The Lord, our Lord, to be ;
But lo, he doth refuse the same,
  No temp'ral Crown would he.

And now transfigur'd on the Mount,
  Behold your dearest Lord,
While *Moses* and *Elias* talk
  With him----a Voice is heard :

From Heav'n it's heard, from Heav'n it came,
  It was no fancy'd Dream ;
" This is my well-beloved Son,
  " Let all the Earth hear him.

And now to *Cæsar* he did pay,
  A Tribute then and there :
A bright Example unto all
  That loyal Subjects are.

A certain Village now there was
  Of great *Samaria*,
Who did refuse to entertain
  Sweet *Jesus* in his Way.

L A

As to *Jerusalem* he went,
  Wherefore his Friends desire,
That down from Heaven he would call
  For a consuming Fire.

But lo the merciful and kind
  Redeemer, them reprov'd,
And show'd, a tender-hearted Christ
  His Creatures better lov'd.

And now the *Seventy* are sent forth,
  Who go by two and two,
To teach and preach, and Miracles
  To work, where-e'er they go.

And now to pray he teacheth them,
  And who can teach like him?
In whom the Spirit of God doth dwell,
  And hath forever been.

Another famous Miracle
  Our glorious Lord displays;
In raising *Lazarus* from the Grave,
  Where he had lain four Days.

Zacheus

Zaccheus he now climbs a Tree,
　To see the blessed Lord,
And instantly converted is
　By his most powerful Word.

On *Bartimeus*, poor and blind,
　The Lord did Pity take,
And did restore to him his Sight,
　For his great Mercy's Sake.

And now behold triumphantly
　Christ to *Jerusalem* rides,
Where Multitudes their Garments spread,
　And some *Hosanna* cry'd.

And now being near the City come,
　He weeps, and sighs, and mourns,
And tells the sore Destruction,
　That swiftly on them comes.

And then into the Temple goes,
　And casts the Traders out,
And cures the Blind, and heals the Lame,
　And makes the Dumb to shout.

　　　　　　　　　　And

And as sweet Jesus walk'd along,
   A Fig-tree he espies,
And for it's barren Fruitlesness
   He curs'd it, and it dies.

And now the first Day being come,
   Of the unleavened Bread,
The *Jews* in mighty Numbers were
   Together gathered

And then the paschal Lamb was slain,
   And Jesus as we hear,
The Passover he then did eat
   With his Disciples there

And

And then the Lord did institute
  The sacramental Feast,
Of his dear Body, and his Blood,
  For all his gracious Guests.

And now to shew his humble Mind,
  A Grace so good and meet,
He condescendeth then to wash
  His poor Disciples Feet.

But O behold the self same Night,
  Sweet Jesus is betray'd
By *Judas*, that accursed Wretch,
  And unto *Pilate* led.

Where he is mock'd and buffetted,
  And likewise spit upon,
By the base Soldiers that were there,
  Who dragged him along.

O Heav'ns be ye astonish'd now,
  O Earth a trembling stand,
To see God's dear and darling Son,
  Smote with accursed Hands.

To

o see his dear and lovely Face,
  Which like an Angel shone,
By base, vile, filthy, wretched Men
  Most cruelly spit on.

And now behold the Lord is brought
  To *Pilate* to be try'd,
And hastily and wrongfully
  Judg'd to be crucify'd.

No sooner said, but lo he's haul'd
  Away to *Calvary*,
A cruel and accursed Death,
  Upon the Cross to die.

At which sad Sight the Sun withdrew
  It's bright and dazling Light,
And Darkness cover'd all the Land,
  As tho' it had been Night.

And

And now my Lambs attend the Voice
   Of Chrift in's Agony;
My God, My God, O wherefore haft
   Thou now forsaken me,

For all his Pangs, and Thirft, and Groans,
   And Sorrows which he felt,
He made his Soul even like to Wax
   In his dear Bowels melt.

Were all for you, my Children dear;
   For you he wept and cry'd,
For you figh'd, for you he groan'd,
   For you he freely dy'd.

An ancient Type being now fulfill'd,
   And to a Wonder done,
Of faithful aged *Abraham*,
   In offering up his Son.

                    But

Abraham offering up his Son *Isaac.*

But O amidſt his mighty Thirſt,
  And delorous Out-cry,
They gave him Vinegar and Gall,
  Who was exceeding dry

But hear---the Lord repeats his Cry,
  Jeſus the Lord of Hoſts ;
And after having cry'd aloud,
  He yielded up the Ghoſt.

Behold the Rocks in Pieces rend,
  The Earth did quake likewiſe.
And Saints which ſlept beneath the Clods,
  In Numbers did ariſe.

Amazing Sight ! dear Lambs comes ſee;
  Your deareſt Lord is ſlain,
And hanging on a curſed Tree,
  His Body doth remain.

The Blood ſtream'd down his precious
  His lovely Hands and Feet,   (Head.
In one moſt pure and purple Gore;
  They altogether meet.

Behold

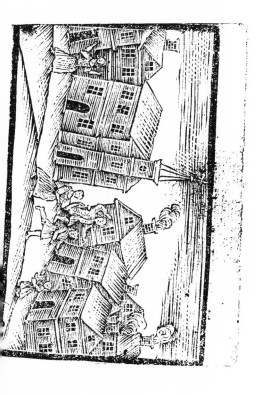

Behold his dear and lovely Head
    Fell on his bleeding Breaſt ;
And all to bring his little Lambs
    To an eternal Reſt.

Now *Joſeph*, a great Man of Fame,
    His lovely Corps doth crave,
And carefully inters it in
    His own peculiar Grave.

Yea, come dear Souls behold the Place,
    Where Jeſus lay when dead,
A Sheet in-wrap'd the Son of God,
    A Napkin bound his Head.

A Watch is ſet, a Guard procur'd,
    To keep our Saviour there,
Who lo, as dead Men they became,
    When *Gabriel* did appear.

Who to attend upon his Lord,
    With Angels many more,
Now ope the dark and ſilent Vault,
    And ſit down at the Door.

                  And

And now behold your Saviour rife,
   Who conquer'd when he fell,
And at his glorious Chariot Wheels
   Led captive Death and Hell.

Which joyful News the Angels told,
   To holy Women then,
That Chrift who lately was interr'd,
   Had now arofe again.   And

And for a Witneſs to the Truth
   Of what they did declare,
The riſen Jeſus graciouſly
   To *Mary* did appear.

And after that to many more,
   To many at one Time,
And to aſſure them it was he,
   With them he pleas'd to dine.

And after having kindly ſupp'd
   With his beloved Ones,
His dear Diſciples,---lo he comes
   To *Olivet* with them.

And then deſires them to wait,
   Even at *Jeruſalem*,
'Till he ſhould ſend the Holy Ghoſt,
   As he had promis'd them.

And then commands them to go forth,
   To teach and to baptize
All Nations that believe on him ;
   And bleſſeth them likewiſe.

And

And while they ſtedfaſtly beheld
   The glorious Lord of Light,
He's taken up, and lo a Cloud
   Receives him out of Sight.

And while, with fixed Eyes, they gaze
   On their aſcending King,
Behold two Men ſtand by in white,
   And theſe ſweet Tidings bring.

Ye Men of *Galilee*, ſay they,
   Why ſtand ye here and gaze,
This Jeſus which was took from you,
   He will not ſtay always.

But in like glorious Manner ſhall
   As you have ſeen him go,
Come down again, aſſure your ſelves
   It ſhall be even ſo.

And now behold your Lord aſcend
   To his eternal Throne,
And by the Father's glorious Hand
   In Royalty ſet down.

                            Set

Set down upon his royal Seat,
    The Father had prepar'd ;
With glorious Proclamation which
    Thro' all the Heav'ns was heard.

Worship him, ye God's Angels all,
    Which swiftly they obey ;
And all the Host their glorious Crowns,
    At Jesus Feet they lay.

Methinks I hear the Heaven's ring
    With Hallelujah's now,
And see the Saints in Multitudes
    Before their Saviour bow.

To God, the glorious God on high,
    They lovely Anthems raise ;
To him that sits upon the Throne,
    And to the Lamb give Praise.

And now, dear Lambs, what look ye for ?
    But soon he'll come again,
In royal Pomp and Trumpets sound,
    To judge a World of Men.
                            The

The Trump which *Gabriel* shall sound,
  Will be so shrill and clear,
That every Soul in Heav'n and Earth,
  The awful Voice will hear.

Then shall the Dead be made to hear
  The Judge's powerful Voice;
The Wicked shriek, the Sinners cry,
  But all the Saints rejoice.

For all the Dead, both small and great,
  Shall stand before the Bar,
And when the Judgment 's summed up
  Their various Sentence' hear.

" My Father's blessed Ones now come,
  (Saith the most just and true)
" Inherit the blest Kingdom which
  " I have prepar'd for you.

But O against all christless Ones,
  What Heart can hear me tell;
Depart from me ye cursed Souls,
  " Into the Fire of Hell.

                    And

And now, dear Children, for whose Sakes
  This little Book I've penn'd,
O be entreated now to make
  Your Judge your dearest Friend.

Receive him for your Prophet, Priest,
  And for your glorious King ;
Act Faith upon this blessed Christ
  And bless your God for him.

Keep close to his most just Commands,
  In all Things please him well ;
Then happy it will be with you
  When Thousands go to Hell.

Where they in Torments lift their Eyes
  Amidst devouring Flames,
While you eternal Praise shall sing,
  To GOD and to the LAMB.

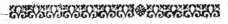

Delight

Delight in the LORD JESUS.

WHEN abfent my dear Saviour is,
　　All Things within me feem amifs;
But when my Jefus he is nigh,
I have moft fweet Felicity.

If my dear Saviour fpeaks not Peace,
Not the whole World can give me Eafe;
But when he fays, Dear Soul I'm thine,
It cheers me more than richeft Wine.

If my dear Saviour doth but frown,
In Depths of Sorrow I'm caft down;
But if he fmiles, nor Earth or Hell,
That can my Light and Joy expell.

If my dear Saviour hides his Face,
I find no Reft in any Place;
But if he looks from Heav'n on me,
My Joys run deep as any Sea.

If my dear Saviour doth withdraw,
I tremble and I ftand in awe;
But if his Prefence me fupport,
I'm fix'd as firm as any Rock.

If

If my dear Saviour lets me fall,
My Sins I to remembrance call ;
But if he keeps me on my Way,
I Joy and Triumph all the Day.

If he let loose the wicked One,
I feel as if I were undone ;
But if he binds the Lion fast,
I then enjoy a sweet Repast.

If Death he let but look on me,
I fear then my Mortality ;
But if he shows his Face again,
I soon get Ease from Fear or Pain.

Nay, should pale Death now come indeed
With all his Fierceness, Haste and Speed,
I fear him not, I him defy,
If my sweet Jesus is but nigh.

Yea, tho' thro' Death's dark Shades I pass
I'll sing each Moment of my Glass,
Redeeming Grace, redeeming Love,
'Till I shall sing free Grace above.

HYMN

HYMN II.

Abfence of CHRIST intolerable.

THine Abfence, Lord, makes me to cry,
 Come quickly, Lord, or I fhall die :
If long my Lord doth ftay away,
Like lonefome Night becomes my Day.

 The beft of Creatures can't afford,
Such Comforts as thy Prefence, Lord :
O dreadful Cafe ! unheard of fad,
When abfent is my Saviour God.

 I round the Univerfe may roll,
And rove about from Pole to Pole ;
But O no Comfort there 's for me,
If my dear Jefus abfent be.

 The Devil throws his fiery Darts,
And wicked Ones do act their parts,
To ruin me when Chrift is gone.
And if he leave me all alone   My

My Lufts they rage, Corruptions fwell,
As if they'd drive me down to Hell.
Yea, helplefs alfo I become,
As any mortal crawling Worm.

Each Blaft of Wind that blows on me,
Seems like the ftrong or raging Sea,
I am fo weak, I am fo fmall ;
Yea I have now no Strength at all.

But if my Lord around me ftay,
I drive all Cares and Fears away ;
Yea, tho' an Hoft engage 'gainft me,
In my Lord's Strength I'd make 'em flee.

In me my deareft Lord doth fee
Nothing but Sin and Mifery ;
For by the Fall I am undone,
And fo is every Woman's Son.

But if my Lord in Grace appear,
He makes me lovely bright and fair ;
If he to Wafhing but begin,
He'll foon deftroy my Guilt and Sin.

If

If he his Garment spread o'er me,
My God in me no Guilt will see;
If he this Garden doth but dress,
'Twill bring forth Fruits of Righteousness.

If he then call and bid me come,
Like Roe I leap, like Hart I run;
If he doth call my Soul away,
I in this World don't want to stay,
But fly as on a Cherub's Wing,
To my dear Christ, my God, my King.

❀❀❀❀❀❀❀❀❀❀❀❀❀❀❀❀❀❀❀❀

The Child's Body of DIVINITY.

ADAM by's Fall bro't Death on all.
By his foul Sin we've ruin'd been.
Christ Jesus come to ransom some.
Dare any say this an't the Way.
Every one to him may come.
For if they do, he'll Mercy show.
Great Grace likewise, to their Surprize.

Heaven

Heaven herein view, and Glory too.
Jesus with Charms, in Faith's strong Arms.
Knowledge and Skill to do his Will.
Love great and strong, to God and Man.
Mercy and Peace which ne'er shall cease.
Near sweet Address, and great Success.
Our Lord unto, whene'er we go.
Putting our Trust, in Christ the Just.
Quickning Grace, he'll give always.
Receiving all, both great and small.
Sincerely who to him do go.
Turning from Sin, tho' vile you've been,
Unto the Lord and Saviour God.
Whoever will, Christ sayeth still,
Xcludeth none that to him come;
Young old and all, he now doth call.
Zealously therefore, accept, adore.
& happy be eternally.

FINIS.

The School of Good Manners

Bibliographical Note:

This facsimile has been
made from a copy in
The Beinecke Library
of Yale University
(Is94.t1.2)

The School of

Good Manners.

CONTAINING

I. Twenty mixt Precepts.

II One Hundred and Sixty Three Rules for Childrens Behaviour.

III. Good Advice for the Ordering of their Lives; With a Baptiſmal Covenant.

IV. Eight wholeſome Cautions.

V. A ſhort, plain, & Scriptural Catechiſm

VI Principles of the Chriſtian Religion

VII. Eleven ſhort Exhortations.

VIII Good Thoughts for Children; A compendious Body of Divinity; An Alphabet of uſeful Copies; and *Cyprian's* Twelve Abſurdities, &c.

The Fifth Edition

New-London,
Printed & Sold by T. & J. Green,
1 7 5 4.

A B C D E F G
H I J K L M N
O P Q R S T
U V W X Y Z

a b c d e f g h i j
k l m n o p q r ſ s
t u v w x y z &

a b c d e f g h i j
k l m n o p q r ſ s
t u v w x y z &

𝕬 𝕭 𝕮 𝕯 𝕰 𝕱 𝕲 𝕳
𝕴 𝕵 𝕶 𝕷 𝕸 𝕹 𝕺 𝕻 𝕼
𝕽 𝕾 𝕿 𝖀 𝖁 𝖂 𝖃 𝖄 𝖅

a b c d e f g h i j
k l m n o p q r s
ſ s t u v w x y z

The Preface.

IT is acknowleged by (almost) every One, That a Good Carriage in Children is an Ornament, not only to Themselves, *but also to* Those whom they Descend *from. When* David (*while he was but a Lad or Youth*) *behaved himself Wisely, the KING Observing of him. said,* Whose Son is this Youth? Enquire — whose Son the Stripling is. 1 *Sam*. xvii. 55, So that *his Parents were Honoured by his good Carriage. Whereas Children of but a mean, careless or* ill *Bree*ding, *brings* Disgrace *on their* Parents, *as well as* Contempt *on* Themselves.

This

This Little Book is Composed for the Help of Parents, in Teaching their Children how to carry it in their Places, during their Minority. [*And 'tis humbly recommended to* School-Masters, *to introduce it into their Schools, as what is* (tho't by some) *proper to be Taught there, and might be very* Profitable] *For we Read,* Prov. xxii. 6, Train up a Child in the Way he should go, and when he is Old he will not depart from it.

The following Institutions were Compiled (chiefly) *by Mr.* ELEAZER MOODEY, *Late a Famous* School-Master *in* Boston, &c. Four *Editions thereof, have been Printed and Sold; and 'tis* hoped *that Parents will* so *befriend this* Edition *also, as to* Inculcate *and* Encourage *their Children, in the* Observation *of what is here Emitted.*

T. GREEN,

THE

SCHOOL

OF GOOD

Manners.

CHAP. I

Containing Twenty mixt Precepts.

1 **F**Ear God & Believe in CHRIST.
   2 Honour the King.
    3 Reverence thy Parents.
    4 Submit to thy Superiors.
5 Despise not thy Inferiors.
6 Be Courteous with thy Equals.
7 Pray daily and devoutly.
8 Converse with the good.
9 Imitate not the wicked.
10 Hear diligently to Instruction
11 Be very desirous of Learning.
      A 3   12 Love

12 Love the School.

13 Be always Neat and Cleanly.

14 Study Vertue and Embrace it.

15 Provoke no Body.

16 Love thy School-Fellows.

17 Please thy Master.

18 Let not Play Entice thee.

19 Restrain thy Tongue.

20 Covet future Honour, which only Vertue & Wisdom can Procure.

CHAP. II.

Containing One Hundred & Sixty Three Rules for Childrens Behaviour, viz. At the Meeting-House; at Home; at the Table; in Company; in Discourse, at the School; when Abroad, and when among Other Children: With an Admonition to them.

§. I. *Of Childrens Behaviour at the Meeting-House.*

1 **D**Ecently walk to thy Seat or Pew; run not nor go wantonly.

2 Sit

2 Sit where thou art Ordered by thy Superiors; Parents or Masters.

3 Shift not Seats, but continue in the Places where your Superiors order you

4 Lend thy Place for the easing of any one that stands near thee.

5 Keep not a Seat too long that is Lent thee by *another*, but being eased thyself restore it to him that lent it to thee.

6 Talk not in the Meeting-house, Especially in the time of Prayer or Preaching.

7 Fix thine Eye upon the Minister, let it not wildly wander to gaze upon any *person or thing*.

8 Attend diligently to the words of the Minister; Pray with him when he Prayes, at least in thy Heart; and while he Preacheth listen that thou mayest Remember.

9 Be not hasty to run out of the Meeting-house when the Worship is ended, as if thou wer't weary of being there.

10 **Walk**

10 Walk Decently and Soberly
Home, without haft or Wantonn-
ness ; thinking upon what you have
been hearing

---

§. II. *Of Childrens Behaviour when
at Home.*

1 MAke a Bow always when
you come Home, and be
immediately Uncovered.

2 Be never Covered at Home, efpe-
cially before thy Parents or Strangers.

3 Never Sit in the Prefence of
thy Parents without bidding, tho'
no Stranger be prefent.

4 If thou paffeft by thy Parents,
at any Place where thou feeft them,
when either by themfelves or with
Company, Bow towards them.

5 If thou art going to *fpeak to thy Pa-
rents* & fee them engag'd in difcourfe
with *Company*, draw back & leave thy
Bufinefs until afterwards ; but if thou
muft fpeak, be fure to Whifper.

6 Never

6 Never speak to thy Parents without some Title of Respect, *viz.* Sir, Madam &c. according to their quality

7 Approach near thy Parents at no time without a Bow.

8 Dispute not, nor delay to Obey thy Parents Commands.

9 Go not out of Doors without thy Parents leave, and return within the time by them Limited.

10 Come not into the Room where thy Parents are with Strangers, unless thou art called, and then decently ; and at bidding go out : or if Strangers come in while thou art with them, it is Manners, with a Bow to withdraw.

11 Use Respectful & Courteous, but not Insulting or Domineering Carriage or Language towards the Servants.

12 Quarrel not nor Contend with thy Brethren or Sisters, but live in Love, Peace and Unity.

13 Grumble not nor be *discontented* at any thing thy Parents *order, speak* or *do*.

14 Bear

14 Bear with Meekneſs & Patience, and withoutMurmuring or Sullenneſs, thy Parents Reproofs or Corrections: Nay, tho' it ſhould ſo happen that they be cauſleſs or undeſerved.

---

§ III. *Of Childrens behavier at the Table.*

1 COme not to the Table without having your Hands and Face Waſhed, and your Head Combed.

2 Sit not down till thou art bidden by thy Parents or other Superiors.

3 Be ſure thou never ſitteſt down till a Bleſſing be deſired, and then in thy due Place.

4 Offer not to carve for thy ſelf, or to take any thing tho' it be that which thou doſt greatly deſire.

5 Aſk not for any thing, but tarry till it be offered thee.

6 Find no fault with any thing that is given thee.

7 When thou haſt Meat given thee, be not the firſt that begins to eat.

8 Speak

8 Speak not at the Table : if thy Superiors be difcourfing, meddle not with the matter ; but be filent, except you are fpoken unto.

9 If thou wanteft any thing from the Servants, call to them foftly.

10 Eat not too faft, or with a greedy behavior.

11 Eat not too much, but moderately.

12 Eat not fo flow as to make others wait for thee.

13 Make not a noife with thy Tongue, Mouth, Lips or Breath, either in eating or drinking.

14 Stare not in the Face of any one (efpecially thy Superior) at the Table.

15 Greafe not thy Fingers or Napkin more than Neceffity requires.

16 Bite not thy Bread, but break it ; but not with flovingly Fingers, nor with the fame wherewith thou takeft up thy Meat.

17 Dip not thy Meat in the Sauce

18 Take not Salt with a greafie Knife:

19 Spit

19 Spit not, Cough not, nor blow thy Nose at the Table, if it may be avoided : but if there be necessity do it aside ; and without much noise.

20 Lean not thy Elbow on the Table, or on the back of thy Chair.

21 Stuff not thy Mouth so as to fill thy Cheeks, be content with smaller mouthfuls.

22 Blow not thy Meat, but with patience wait until it be cool.

23 Sup not Broth at the Table ; but eat it with a Spoon.

24 Smell not of thy Meat, nor put it to thy Nose : turn it not the other side upward to view it upon thy Plate or Trencher.

25 Throw not any thing under the Table.

26 Hold not thy Knife upright in thy hand, but sloping, and lay it down at thy right Hand, with the Blade upon thy Plate.

27 Spit

27 Spit not forth any thing that is not convenient to be Swallowed, as the stones of Plumbs, Cherries, or such like, but with thy left hand, neatly move them to the side of thy Plate, or Trencher.

28 Fix not thine Eyes upon the Plate or Trencher of another, or upon the Meat on the Table.

29 Lift not up thine Eyes, nor roul them about while thou art drinking.

30 Foul not the Napkin all over, but at one corner only.

31 Bend thy Body a little downwards to thy Plate, when thou movest any thing that is Sauce to thy Mouth.

32 Look not Earnestly on any one that is Eating.

33 Foul not the Table-Cloth.

34 Gnaw not bones at the Table, but clean them with thy knife, (unless they be very small ones) and hold them not with a whole hand, but with two fingers:

B

35 Drink

35 Drink not nor speak with any thing in thy Mouth.

36 Put not a bit into thy Mouth till the former be swallowed.

37 Before and after thou drinkest, wipe thy Lips with thy Napkin.

38 Pick not thy Teeth at the Table, unless holding up thy Napkin before thy Mouth with thine other hand.

39 Drink not till thou hast quite Emptied thy Mouth, nor drink often.

40 Frown not, nor Murmur if there be any thing at the Table which thy Parents or Strangers with them eat of, while thou thy self hast none given thee

41 As soon as thou shalt be moderately Satisfied ; or whensoever thy Parents think meet to bid thee, rise up from the Table, tho' others thy Superiors sit still.

42 When thou risest from the Table, take away thy Plate ; and having made a Bow at the side of the Table where thou sattest, withdraw, removing
ing

ing alfo thy Seat (if removeable.)

43 When Thanks are to be return-
ed after Eating, return to thy Place,
and ftand reverently till it be done ;
then with a Bow withdraw out of the
Room, leaving thy Superiors to them-
felves (unlefs thou art bidden to ftay.)

§ IV. *Of Childrens Behaviour when in Company.*

1 ENter not into the Company of
Superiors without command
or calling, nor without a Bow.

2 Sit not down in Prefence of
Superiors without bidding.

3 Put not thy hand in the prefence
of others to any part of thy Body,
not ordinarily difcovered.

4 Sing not nor Hum in thy mouth,
while thou art in Company.

5 Play not wantonly like a Mi-
mick, with thy Fingers or Feet.

6 Stand not Wriggling with thy Body
hither & thither, but fteady & upright

7 In Coughing or Neefing, make as little Noife as poffible.

8 If thou canft not avoid Yawning, fhut thy mouth with thine *hand* or *bankerchief* before it, turning thy face afide

9 When thou bloweft thy Nofe, let thy Hankerchief be ufed, and make not a noife in fo doing.

10 Gnaw not thy Nails, pick them not, nor bite them with thy Teeth.

11 Spit not in the Room, but in the Corner, and rub it with thy Foot, or rather go out and do it abroad.

12 Lean not upon the Chair of a Superior ftanding behind him.

13 Spit not upon the Fire, nor fit too wide with thine Knees at it.

14 Sit not with thy Legs Croffed, but keep 'em firmly fettl'd, & thy *feet even*

15 Turn not thy Back to any, but place thy felf fo conveniently that none may be behind thee.

16 Read not Letters, Books nor other Writings in Company, unlefs
there

there be necessity, & thou askest leave.

17 Touch not nor look upon the Books or Writings of any one, unless the Owner invite or desire thee.

18 Come not near when another Reads a Letter or any other Paper.

19 Let thy *Countenance* be moderately chearful, neither Laughing nor Frowning.

20 Laugh not aloud, but silently Smile upon occasion.

21 Stand not before Superiors with thine hands in thy Pockets; scratch not thy head, wink not with thine Eyes, but modestly be looking strait before thee.

22 Walking with thy Superior in the House or Garden, give him the Right (or Upper) Hand, & Walk not even with him, *Cheek-by-jole* ; but a little behind him, yet not so distant as that it shall be troublesome to him to speak to thee, or hard for thee to hear.

23 Look not boldly or wishfully in the Face of thy Superior.

24 To

24 To look upon one in Company and immediately whisper to another, is unmannerly.

25 Whisper not in Company.

26 Be not among Equals froward and fretful, but gentle and affable.

§. V. *Of Childrens Behavior in their Discourse.*

AMong Superiors speak not till thou art spoken to, and bid to speak Hold not thine *hand*, nor any *thing else* before thy *mouth* when thou *speakest.*

3 Come not over near to the Person thou speakest to .

4 If thy Superior speak to thee while thou sitest, stand up before thou givest any answer.

5 Sit not down till thy *Superior* bid thee.

6 Speak neither very loud, or too low

7 Speak clear, not stammering, stumbling nor drawling.

8 Answer not one that is speaking to thee until he hath done.

9 Loll

9 Loll not when thou art speaking to a Superior, or spoken to by him.

10 Speak not without, *Sir*, or some other Title of Respect, which is due to him to whom thou speakest.

11 Strive not with Superiors in Argument or Discourse; but easily submit thine Opinion to their Assertions.

12 If thy *Superior* speak any thing wherein thou knowest he is mistaken, correct not nor contradict him, or grin at the hearing of it; but pass over the Error without notice or interruption.

13 Mention not frivolous or little *things* before *grave Persons* or *Superiors*

14 If thy Superior drawl or hesitate in his words, pretend not to help him out, or to prompt him.

15 Come not too near Two that are whispering or speaking in secret, much less to ask 'em about what they confer.

16 When thy Parent or Master speak to any Person, speak not thou, nor hearken to them:

17 **If**

17 If thy Superior be relating a Story, say not I have heard it before, but attend to it, as if it were to thee altogether new : Seem not to question the Truth of it ; If he tell it not right, snigger not, nor endeavour to help him out or add to his Relation.

18 If any Immodest or Obscene thing be spoken in thy hearing, smile not at it, but settle thy Countenance as tho' thou did'st not hear it.

19 Boast not in Discourse of thine own wit or doings.

20 Beware thou utter not any thing hard to be believ'd.

21 Interrupt not any one that speaks, tho' thou be his Familiar.

22 Coming into Company, whilst any Topic is discoursed on, ask not what was the preceding talk, but hearken to the remainder.

23 Speaking of any distant Person, it is rude & unmannerly to point at him

24 Laugh not in, or at thy own Story, Wit or Jest.　　　　25 Use

25 Use not any Contemptuous cr ReproachfulLanguage to any person, tho' very mean or inferior.

26 Be not over earnest in talking to justify and avouch thy own sayings.

27 Let thy words be modest about those things which only concern thee.

28 Repeat not over again the words of a Superior that asketh thee a Question, or talketh to thee.

---

§. VI. *Of Childrens Behaviour at the School.*

1 BOw at coming in pulling off thy Hat; especially if thy Master or Usher be in the School.

2 Loiter not, but immediately take thine own Seat; and move not from one Place to another, till School-time be over.

3 If any Stranger come into the School, rise up and bow, and sit down in thy Place again; keeping a profound Silence.

4 If

4 If thy Master be Discoursing in the School with a Stranger, stare not confidently on them, nor hearken to their Talk.

5 Interrrupt not thy Master while a Stranger or Visitant is with him, with any Question, Request or Complaint ; but refer any such matter until he be at leasure.

6 At no time Quarrel or Talk in the School, but be quiet, peaceable and silent. Much less may'st thou deceive thy self, in trifling away thy precious time in Play.

7 If thy Master speak to thee, rise up and bow ; making thine Answer standing.

8 Bawl not aloud in making Complaints. A Boys Tongue should never be heard in the School, but in answering a Question, or saying his Lesson.

9 If a Stranger speak to thee in School, stand up and answer with respect and ceremony, both of word

and

and gesture, as if thou spakest to thy Master.

10 Make not haste out of School, but soberly go when thy turn comes, without noise or hurry.

11 Go not rudely home thro' the Street, stand not talking with Boys to delay thee, but go quietly home, and with all convenient haste.

12 When it is time to return to School again, be sure to be there in season, and not loiter at home whilst your Master is at School.

13 Divulge not to any Person whatsoever elsewhere, any thing that hath passed in the School, either spoken or done.

§. VII. *Of Childrens Behaviour when Abroad.*

1 GO not Singing, Whistling nor Hollowing along the Street.

2 Quarrel not with any Body thou meetest or dost overtake.

3 Affront

3 Affront none, especially thy Elders, by word or deed.

4 Jeer not any Person whatsoever.

5 Always give the Right Hand to your Superiors, when either you meet or walk with them; and mind also to give them the Wall, in meeting or walking with them; for that is the Upper Hand, though in walking your Superior should be at your Left Hand. But when Three Persons walk together, the middle place is the most Honourable: And a Son may walk at his Fathers Right Hand, when his Younger Brother walks at his Left.

6 Give thy Superior leave to pass before thee in any narrow place, where Two persons cannot pass at once.

7 If thou go with thy Parents, Master, or any Superior, go not wantonly, nor even with them; but a little behind them.

8 Pay thy Respects to all thou meetest of thine Acquaintance or Friends.

9 Pull

9 Pull off thine Hat to Perfons of Defert, Quality or Office ; shew thy Reverence, to them by bowing thy Body when thou feeft them ; and if it be the King, a Prince, Noble, Governour, Magiftrate, Juftice of the Peace, Minifter or Deacon, &c. ftay thy felf until they be paffed by thee.

10 If a Superior fpeak to thee in the Street anfwer him with thy head Uncovered ; and put not on thy Hat until he either go from thee, or bid thee once and again be covered ; take not leave at the firft bidding, but with a bow, [*by no means, Sir,*] modeftly refufe it.

11 Run not haftily in the Street, or go too flowly ; wag not to & fro, nor ufe any antick or wanton pofture, either of thy Head, Hands Feet or Body.

12 Stare not at every Unufual Perfon or Thing thou feeft.

13 Throw not any thing in the Street, as Dirt, Stones, &c.

C

14 If

14 If thou meetest the Scholars of any other School, jeer not nor affront them, but shew them love and respect, and quietly let them pass along.

15 Especially affront not the Master of another School, but rather, if thou knowest him, or if he live either near thine House or School, uncover thy Head to him, & bowing pass by him.

---

§. VIII. *Of their Behaviour among other Children.*

1 AS near as may be Converse not with any but those that are good, sober and vertuous. *Evil communications corrupt good Manners.*

2 Be not Quarrelsome, but rather patiently take, than mischievously occasion any manner of wrong.

3 Reprove thy Companions as oft as there shall be occasion, for any evil, wicked, unlawful or indecent Action or Expression.

4 Give always Place to him that Excelleth

celleth thee in Quality. Age or Learning

5 Be willing to take thofe Words or Actions as Jefting, which thou haft reafon to believe were defigned for fuch; and fret not at thy Companions innocent Mirth.

6 If thy Companion be a little too grofs or farcaftical in fpeaking, yet ftrive not to take notice of it, or moved at all therewith.

7 Abufe not thy Companion either by Word or Deed·

8 Deal juftly among Boys thy Equals, as folicitoufly as if thou wert a Man with Men, and about Bufinefs of higher importance.

9 Be not Selfifh altogether, but kind, free and generous to others.

10 Jog not the Table or Defk on which another Writes.

11 At play make not thy Cloathes, Hands or Face dirty or nafty, nor fit upon the ground.

12 Avoid finful and unlawful Re-
C 2   creations,

creations, and all such as prejudice the welfare of Body or Mind.

13 Scorn not, laugh not at any for their natural infirmities of Body or Mind ; nor because of them affix to any a vexing Title of Contempt and Reproach. But pity such as are so visited, and be thankful that you are otherwise distinguished & favoured.

14 Adventure not to talk with thy Companion about thy *Superiors*, to raise discourse reflecting upon, or touching anothers Parents or Masters ; to publish any thing of thine own Family or Houshold affairs. Children must meddle only with the affairs of Children.

§. IX. *Containing an Admonition to Children.*

CHildren, These are the chief of those Rules of Behavior the Observation *whereof* will deliver you from the disgraceful Titles of Sordid and Clownish, and intail upon the mention

of

of you, the honour of genteel & well-bred Children : For there is scarce a sadder sight, than a clownish and unmannerly Child.   Avoid therefore with the greatest diligence so vile an Ignominy. Be humble, submissive & obedient, to those whose Authority by Nature or Providence hath a just claim to your Subjection : Such are *Parents, Masters,* or *Tutors,* whose Commands & Laws have no other tendency than your truest good. Be always obsequious and respectful, never bold, insolent or sawcy, either in Words or Gestures. Let your Body be on every occasion pliable, & ready to manifest in due & becoming Ceremonies, the inward Reverence you bear towards those above you. By this means, by a timely and early accustoming your selves to a sweet & spontaneous Obedience in your lower Station and Relations, your minds being habituated to that which is so indispensibly

your

your duty, the task of Obedience in further Relations will be performed with the greater Ease & Pleasure. When it shall please God that you come to riper Years, and under the circumstance of Servants, pay Homage to your Masters and Mistresses ; and at length if it shall seem good to the Divine Providence, that you arrive at Manhood, & become Members of the Common-Wealth, there will remain in your well managed Minds no presumptuous Folly, that may in the least prompt or tempt you to be other than Faithful, Obedient and Loyal Subjects.

Be kind, pleasant & loving, not cross or churlish to your Equals. And in thus behaving your selves, all persons will exceedingly desire your familiar Acquaintance: Every one will be ready & willing (upon opportunity) to serve & assist you. Your Friends will be no fewer than all that know you, & observe the excellence & sweetness of

your

your deportment. This practice also (by inducing an habit of Obliging) will fit you for Converse & Society, and facilitate & advantage your dealing with Men in riper Years.

Be meek, courteous and affable to your Inferiors, not proud or scornful. To be Courteous to the Meanest is a true *Index* of a great and generous Mind. [But the insulting & scornful Gentleman, usually hath been himself originally Low, Ignoble or Beggarly ; makes himself to his Equals ridiculous, and by his Inferiors is repaid with scorn and hatred]

By carefully observing these methods of Life, your Superiors will indeed Esteem you ; your Inferiors Honour and Admire you ; your Equals Delight in & love you ; all that Know and Observe you, shall Praise and Respect you : Your Example shall be propounded as a Pattern of Ingenuity and obliging Behaviour. You shall

be

be Valuable and Well-Esteemed in every Time, Station and Circumstance of your Lives: You shall be blest with the Names of good Children, good Scholars, good Servants, good Masters, good Subjects; Praise shall be your Attendance all your lives long, & your Names shall Out-live the Envy of the Grave; the Encomium of every Survivor shall Embalm your *Memory*.

CHAP. III.
Containing §. I. *Good Advice to Children.*

1 BElieve without Doubt that there is a God, that He is most Holy, hating Sin, and that never any shall see Him & taste of His Sweetness, unless they Walk Holy before Him.

2 Be assured that the sacred Scriptures (the *Written Word of God*) are True; and that the things contained therein, will be found to be real Things.

3 If God do open your Eyes & bring you to Salvation, it will be by light let in by the Word.   4 There-

4 Therefore read it, & muse upon it, & never read it without looking up to God to speak to your case out of it.

5 And when you go to hear the word Preached, be sure go to hear God, and listen with Diligence to every Word that is spoken.

6 Make it one main work, & try at it again & again, to Meditate, & in Meditation to conclude what your State is; and to ask both the Lord & your own Consciences concerning your State; and give no rest to either, till you put that great Question out of Question, where you shall spend your Eternity.

7 Be sure that Sin is the greatest Evil in the world; and that no Affliction can hurt us if Sin do not.

8 Examine what your most Especial Sin is, which you shall know from its most frequent rising out of your *Heart*, & bring that before God, and Pray against it day & night; and Resolve against it: For there will be no *Communion*

nion with *God* if this sin *reigns in you·*

9 Study to know Jesus Christ every way, and give God no rest until He Reveals Christ as the most glorious thing to you ; and until you can say, Now I see that all other things are but loss in comparison of Christ.

10 Make a serious Dedication of yourself to him, to be his, and chuse him to be yours ; write your own Covenant and Subscribe it, & satisfie your self with Christ tho' you have nothing else, & give up your self to be ruled by him, & then say thou art my Lord, help me now in the time of my straits.

11 Pray Morning & Evening without fail, and that with all Seriousness ; for those things that you want, and against those things that you fear.

12 Be faithful in your Place & Calling, & let there not the least Unrighteousness lie upon your Consciences.

13 Be diligent to improve Time, and suffer not precious Hours to wast

and

and run away without Improvement.
14 Remember you have awful work to
do, till sin be pardon'd & heaven assur'd

15 Make it part of your daily work
to call your Heart to an Account ; and
do not any Momentary Business with-
out proposing of some grounded End
that will bear you out in it, let the
Event be even what it will.

16 And if you love your Life, beware
of Evil Company, a deadly Mischief ;
rather *none* than ill *ones*, which there be
in every place. Have no fellowship
with 'em, do not keep with 'em if pos-
sible, for the Devil has poison'd many
a man thus. *Keep your self pure.* Be
choice of your Company as of your *life*.
17 Now is the time for you to offer to
the Lord the first Fruits, the Morning
of your Age, the Prime of your Days.
18 Labour to approve your self Ho-
nest before God and men. The way
to be upright is to walk before God.
Set God before you as One that seeth
and

and trieth not only Visible, but secret
tho'ts & secret works. He sees in
the Dark, as well as in the Light.

---

§. II. *A short Baptismal Covenant, to
be Subscribed unto, & kept by Young
Persons for their Use, & Comfort ;
which if seriously & often Reflected
upon and well Considered of, would
tend to the prevention of much Evil,
and be a means to promote much
Joy and Comfort to their Souls.*

I Take God the FATHER, to be my
chiefest Good, and highest End

I take God the SON, to be my
Prince, and Saviour.

I take God the HOLY GHOST, to be
my Sanctifier, Teacher, & Comforter.

I take the Word of GOD to be my
Rule in all my Actions.

And the People of GOD to be my
People in all my Conditions.

I do likewise Devote, and Dedi-
cate unto the LORD, my whole Self,
all

all I am, all I have, and all I can do.

And this I do Deliberately, & as far as I know my own Heart, Sincerely, Freely, & for evermore ; Depending always on the Sovereign Grace of GOD & Merits of the Lord JESUS CHRIST alone, for Affistance and Acceptance.

CHAP. IV.

Containing Eight wholsome Cautions:
I. Of taking God's Name in Vain.

THIS is a Sin that Children are addicted unto ; to say, *O Lord, O God, O Jesus, O Christ, &c.* in their Common Talk, upon every Frivilous Occasion ; but it is expresly forbidden in the Third Commandment : The words of which Command are these, *Thou shalt not take the Name of the Lord thy God in vain : for the Lord will not hold him Guililess that taketh His Name in vain.* Therefore be Warned to take heed of this Sin.

He will not hold him guiltless. i.e. He
D will

will surely hold him *guilty*. To be held guilty before God, Notes two things.

1 To be under the Merit of Everlasting Wrath : by taking God's Name in vain, you deserve the Wrath of the Great and Infinite God.

2 Guilt Notes an Obligation to Wrath · taking God's Name in vain, binds you over to the Judgment of the great Day ; when thou comest to appear before God's Tribunal, and it be Demanded of thee, Guilty, or not Guilty ? This Sin alone will prove you to be really Guilty.

And certainly, however the breakers of this Command may escape punishment here, yet they shall find there is a Judgment.

II. Of *Vain, Idle and Naughty Words.*

THis is another Sin that Children are addicted unto : But our Saviour tells us, Mat. 12. 36. *That every Idle Word that Men shall speak,*
they

they muſt give an account thereof in the *Day of Judgment :* Do you believe this, Children, & will you yet ſpeak Idle words, Vain words, Naughty words ? O have a care of this evil.

III. *Of the Sin of Lying.*

THis is another Sin that Children are addicted unto, and are to be Warned againſt. A Lie, is a ſpeaking an untruth wittingly & willingly, with a purpoſe to deceive. Of Lies there are Three ſorts, *viz.*

An Officious Lie. A Sporting Lie. And a Pernicious Lie.

1. An Officious Lie, is that which is intended to prevent ſome danger, or procure ſome good, either to our Selves or Neighbours. Thus *Rahab* Lied, *Joſh.* 2. 4. And that Woman mentioned in 2 *Sam,* 17. 20.

2. A Sporting Lie, or Lie in Jeſt, is that which is made to make one merry, or to paſs away Precious Time.

3. A Pernicious Lie, is that which is made for some evil, hurtful, dangerous intent against our Neighbour. All these sorts of Lying are Sinful.

A Lying Tongue is one of the things that are an Abomination to the Lord, Prov. 6. 16, 17. *A Proud Look, a Lying Tongue,* &c. And again, Prov. 12. 22. *Lying Lips are an abomination to the Lord.* And Lying is the mark of the Devils Children, Joh. 8, 44. *Ye are of your Father the Devil— He abode not in the truth because there is no truth in him; when he speaketh a Lie, he speaketh of his own; for he is a Liar & the Father of it.* Liars are reckoned among the grossest of Sinners, and must go to the same Hell that they are going to. We are told, Rev. 21. 8. *The Fearful, and Unbelieving, & the Abominable, & Murderers, & Whoremongers, & Sorcerers, & Idolaters, & all* LIARS. *shall have their part in the Lake which burneth with Fire and Brimstone.*

A

A Liar is abhorred both of God &
Man ; he is abhorred of God, as you
were before told, *Lying lips are an a-*
bomination to the Lord, Prov. 12. 22.
He is also abhorred of Man : *David*
could not endure a Liar in his sight,
Psal. 1. 1. 7. *He that worketh deceit*
shall not dwell within my house : he
that telleth lies shall not tarry in my
sight. 'Tis said of *Pomponias* that he
never used Lying, neither could he
with Patience lend his ear to a Liar.
Tenendo was so strict in Judgment, that
he caus'd an Ax to be held over the
Witnesses Head, to execute them out
of hand, if they were taken in a Fals-
hood. If one accustom himself to Ly-
ing he is scarce believ'd when he speaks
True. The Devils Breast (saith *Lu-*
ther) is very fruitful with Lies. *Austin*
hath a Tractate about an Officious
Lie : To tell a Lie for no hurt, but
for good (says he) we are not to do
it, though it were to save all the World.

Thergh

Though some Saints & holy Servants of God have used the Officious Lie, as *Rebecca*, & *Jacob*, *Gen.* 27. 18, 19. And *Abraham*, *Gen.* 20. 2. Yet their Faults were not Recorded for our Imitation, but for our Caution.

IV. *Of Obscene & Wanton Speeches, & Lascivious Songs & Ballads.*

THis is another Sin that Children are addicted to, & to be warned of : This is a Sin that doth greatly Corrupt Youth. The Apostle *Paul* Cautions you against it, *Eph.* 4. 29. *Let no Corrupt Communication proceed out of your mouth.* And Chap. 5. 4. *Neither Filthiness, nor Foolish Talking, nor Jesting,* &c. Have a Care of Lascivious Speeches, and of Unchast and Wanton Songs or Ballads : Take heed, Children, of these things ; for the Practice of them will greatly Debauch you : Therefore you should much rather improve your Time in

Rea ing

Reading the Bible, & other Books of Piety, which have a tendency to make you wife unto Salvation,

V. *Of Profane and Rash Swearing.*

THis is another Vice whereunto Young Men are too much addicted: But expreſly forbidden by our Saviour, Mat. 5. 24 *Swear not at all* (i e. Profanely or Raſhly) *but let your Communication be Yea, yea : Nay, nay : for whatſoever is more than theſe cometh of evil*; i.e. of the Devil that evil one. Have a care of Swearing by Faith, & Troth, *much more* by the Name of God

VI. *Of Profaning the Sabbath-Day.*

SAbbath-breaking is another Sin which Children are too generally prone unto. The Fourth Commandment is, *Remember the Sabbath Day to keep it Holy*. But how contrary hereto is the Practice of very many Children & elder Perſons too ? Oh ! then, have

a

a care of playing upon the Lord's Day,
which is the Christians Sabbath; but do
you spend the whole day in religious
Exercises.   That famous Judge Sir
Matthew Hale, who in a Letter to his
Children in which he gives them di-
rections for the Sanctification of the
Lord's day; says, That he often found
that the due Observation of the duty of
this Day, had ever joyn'd to it a *Blessing*
on the rest of his Time; and the Week
so begun was Blessed and Prosperous
to him : But if on the other side, he
had been Negligent in the duties of
this Day, the rest of the Week was
Unhappy ; so that he could easily
make an Estimate of his Successes, by
the manner of his passing this Day :
and this (*says he*) I do not write lightly,
or inconsiderately, but upon long and
sound Observation and Experience.

A late Writer tells us, that a Friend
of his observing a Woman exposing
Fruit to Sale on the Lords day, advised
her

her to leave that practice & to attend
the Public Worship, and serve God on
His Day. The Woman replied, that
she took more Money on the Lord's
Day, than on any day of the Week, &
that she could not live, if she did not
do thus. To whom it was replied, if
you would leave off this Practice, &
keep the Lords Day holy, attending the
Public Worship; and when you come
home spend the time in Reading the
Scripture, & in Prayer to God, & Prais-
ing Him for his Mercies, God will send
a Blessing on your labours on the rest
of the Week, which you cannot expect
so long as you make a Market of His
Sabbath. The Woman hearkned to
his Advice, & sometime after thanked
him for it: saying she found his words
true; for ever since she kept the *Sab-
bath-day*, she Sold more on *Mondays*
& *Tuesdays* than she used to do all the
Week before. But there is greater
things to be obtained by observing this
holy

holy Day, than Temporal Blessings, *viz.*
Spiritual and Eternal Blessings.

And consider also the Judgments
which have overtook those who have
Profaned that Day : One speaks of
Fourteen Young Persons who on a
Lord's day in the winter time would
go to play at Foot-ball on the Ice, but
that broke under them, & they were
all Drowned. 'Tis reported that two
Young Men belonging to *New-England*
would be so Profane as to ride a Race
on the Lord's day, but when they were
on their Horses Backs, God smote 'em
with a strange kind of Palsey of which
they both died, after they had been for
several Months in a very miserable
Condition. But Sabbath breakers ex-
pose themselves to that which is worse
than any Temporal Judgments, *viz.*
to Spiritual and Eternal Judgments.

VII. *Of Stealing.*

THis is another Sin which Children
are prone unto : tho' 'tis for-
bidden

bidden in the Eighth Commandment. The Eighth Commandment is, *Thou shalt not Steal.* To Steal is to take that which is anothers without their Leave. O! Children, be caution'd against the sin of Stealing : Steal not the value of a Pin from any one ; especially from your Parents or Masters, for to Steal from them is a great sin, tho' some may count it none at all. A Thief is reckoned up among those sinners that shall be shut out of Heaven. 1 Cor. 6. 9. --- *Know ye not that the Unrighteous shall not inherit the kingdom of God. Be not deceived, neither fornicators, nor idolators, nor adulterers, nor effeminate, (i.e.* Self-polluters) *nor abusers of themselvs with mankind, nor* THIEVES, (which are plac'd in the middle of those ungodly ones, as if they were the worst of them all) *nor covetous, nor drunkards, nor revilers, nor extortioners, shall inherit the kingdom of God.*

VIII.

VIII. *Of Disobedience to Parents.*

Disobedience to Parents, is another sin too common among Children, and indeed 'tis a great sin. Obedience to Parents is that which is exprefly required of Children in the fifth Commandment, which is, *Honour thy Father and thy Mother.* But alas, how many Children do violate this great Commandment? Disobedience to Parents is fo foul a fin, as that it is put into that black Catalogue, Rom. 1.29,30,31. *Being filled with all unrighteeufnefs, fornication, wickednefs, coveteoufnefs, malicioufnefs, full of envy, murder, debate, deceit, malignity, whifperers, backbiters, haters of God, defpiteful, proud, boafters, inventers of evil things,* DISOBEDIENT TO PARENTS, *covenant breakers, without natural affection, implacable, unmerciful.* Many that have come to an untimely Death, and that both in the days of old and in our days, in the Land of our

fore-fathers

fore-fathers Sepulchers & in the Land
where we live, have (when the ter-
rors of Death been upon them, and
they just ready to launch out into an
awful Eternity) bitterly lamented &
very much bewailed that God-pro-
voking Sin, *viz.* *Disobedience to their
Parents.* Let Children take heed they
be not found among such ; but let
them always remember that word,
Eph.6.1.*Children, Obey your Parents
in the Lord, for this is right.*

C H A P. V.
*Containing a short, plain, & scriptural
Catechism.*

Q 1. **D**O *you know who is God, &
who made you & us all* ?

A. I know that the Lord he is God,
that he made us, & not we ourselves.

Q 2. *Who is he that hath preserved
you from the Womb hitherto* ?

A. The Lord hath upheld me from
the Womb hitherto, *Pf.*71.5.*Ifa.*44.2

B   Q 3.

Q 3. Whom then are you bound to warship, and serve ?

A. The great God, that hath made, and preserved me, *Psal.* 100. 2,3:

Q 4. When are you to set yourself to this happy work of serving God ?

A. While I am a Child, in the days of my Youth, *Eccl.* 12.1 2 *Tim.* 3.15

Q. 5. What Rule have you to direct you how to serve the Lord ?

A. The Word of God, contained in the old & new Testament, is the only Rule to direct me how to serve the Lord.

Q 6.   What is GOD ?

A. God is a most holy, wise, merciful, just & mighty Spirit, yea he is almighty

Q 7. Are there more Gods than One ?

A. Our God is but One ; the Father of whom are all things ; the Son, Jesus Christ the Saviour, by whom are all things ; and the Holy Spirit of Truth, whom the Father sends in the Son's Name to Sanctify & Comfort.

Q 8. What Works hath God done ?

A. God

A. God made the heavens, & the earth, & the waters; and all that in them is, *Gen* 1. 1. *Exod.* 20. 11.

Q 9. *Whether did God at first, make all things good or bad ?*

A. God made all things very good.

Q 10. *How then came sin, sorrow and death into the World ?*

A. By *Adam*'s Fall, in whom we all sinned, & came short of the glory of God.

Q 11. *What is Sin ?*

A. Sin is any want of conformity unto or transgression of the Law of God.

Q 12. *What do you, and I, deserve for committing of Sin ?*

A. The wages of sin is Death, and the Wrath of GOD, *Rom.* 6. 23 *Gal* 3. 10

Q. 13. *What hopes have you of being delivered from Sin, and so from Death and the Wrath of God.*

A. The Love of God who gave His only begotten Son, that whosoever Believeth in him should not Perish, but have everlasting Life, *Joh.* 3. 16.

Q. 14. *What did Christ the Son of God do in order to the Redeeming Mankind?*

A. Christ became our Surety unto God, so he undertook the curse in our stead, and died to Redeem us from Sin & Wrath, *Heb.* 7. 22. 25. *Gal.* 3. 13.

Q. 15. *Who are they that shall share in these Benefits purchased by Christ?*

A. Such as are convinced of Sin, of Righteousness & of Judgment; and that receive Jesus Christ as their Prophet, Priest & King, *Joh.* 16. 8.

Q. 16. *How must you live if you hope to be saved by Jesus Christ?*

A. I must live in all Purity, cleansing my self from all filthiness of flesh and spirit, perfecting holiness in the fear of God, 1 *Joh.* 3. 2, 3. 1 *Cor.* 7. 1.

Q. 17. *How are you to worship & serve the great God?*

A. I must worship & serve God in spirit & in truth; with all my heart & with all my soul, & with all my might.

Q. 18. *What is the best evidence of your Love to God?*   *A.*

A. The keeping his Commandments, and counting the doing of them a pleasure, *Joh.* 14. 15. 1 *Joh.* 5. 3.

Q. *How many Commandments are there?*

A. There are Ten Commandments.

Q. 20. *What excellent Sum have you of the Christian Faith?*

A. That which usually goes under the name of the Apostles Creed. [Which let the Child now repeat.]

Q 21. *What is the most perfect form of Prayer?*

A. That which Jesus Christ taught his Disciples [Repeat the Lord's Prayer.]

Q. 22. *What are the Sacraments of the New-Testament?*

A. Baptism, as entring into the Church of Christ; and the Lord's Supper, as confirming and comforting us there. *Mat.* 28. 19, 20. *Act.* 2. 42.

Q. 23. *What will become of the wicked after death?*

A. They must be turned into Hell, with all those that forget God, *Psi* 9 17.

Q. 24.

Q. 24. *What also becomes of the godly,
or those that fear God & serve Him ?*

A. They all go to Heaven, & are for
ever solaced in rivers of Pleasures at
God's right Hand, *Mat* 25. 34 *Rev* 2. 10

CHAP. VI.

*Containing Principles of the Christian
Religion ; in which there is a double
advantage to Youth, (1) In that all
the while they are reading of them,
they learn to Read as well as by
reading any other Matter. (2) In that
thereby they are Instructed in the
Grounds & Principles of Religion.*

One G O D.

HAve we not one Father ? hath not
one God created us ? *Mal.* 2. 10
But be not ye called Rabbi : For one
is your Master, even Christ ; and all ye
are Bretheren : And call no man your
Father upon Earth : For One is your
Father which is in Heaven, *Mat* 23. 8, 9.

The Lord he is God ; and there is
none

none elfe befides him, *Deut.* 4. 35

Hear, O Ifrael, The Lord our God is one Lord, *Deut.* 6. 4.

I am the Lord, and there is none elfe befides me, *Ifa.* 45. 5.

An Idol is nothing in the world, and there is none other God but one. To us there is but one God, the Father, of whom are all things, 1 *Cor.* 8. 4.

For there is one God, and there is none other but he, *Mark* 12. 32.

Seeing it is one God, which fhall Juftifie the circumcifion by Faith.

Now a Mediatour is not a Mediatour of One ; but God is One, *Gal.* 3. 20

One Lord, one Faith, one Baptifm ; one God and Father of all, who is above all, & through all, & in you all.

For there is one God, and one Mediatour between God and men, the Man Chrift Jefus, 1 *Tim.* 2. 5.

But the Lord he is the true God, he is the living God, and an everlafting King, *Jer.* 10. 10.

Three

Three Persons in the Godhead; i.e. *the Father, the Son, & the Holy Ghost.*

GO ye therefore and Teach all Nations, Baptizing them in the Name of the Father, and of the Son, and of the Holy Ghost, *Mat.* 28. 19.

There are Three that bear record in Heaven, the Father, the Word, and the Holy Ghost : and these three are ONE, 1 *John* 5. 7.

And Jesus when he was baptized went straightway out of the water : and lo, the Heavens were opened unto him, & he saw the Spirit of God descending like a dove, and lighting upon him. And lo, a Voice from Heaven, saying, This is my beloved Son in whom I am well pleased, *Mat.* 3. 16. 17.

The Grace of our Lord Jesus Christ, and the Love of God, and the Communion of the Holy Ghost, be with you all, Amen, 2 *Cor.* 13. 14.

And I will pray the Father, and he shall give you another Comforter, that

he

he may abide with you for ever : even
the Spirit of Truth,—*Joh.* 14.16.17.

Of the Attributes of G O D.

I. *Of* G O D's *Eternity.*

BUt now is made manifest, and by
the Scriptures of the Prophets,
according to the Commandment of
the everlasting God, made known to
all Nations for the obedience of Faith.

Hast thou not known ? hast thou
not heard, that the everlasting God
the Lord, the Creator of the ends of
the Earth fainteth not, neither is
weary ? there is no searching of his
understanding, *Isa.* 40. 20.

Who hath wrought and done it,
calling the generations from the be-
ginning ? I the Lord the first, and with
the last, I am he, *Isa.* 41. 4.

Before the Mountains were brought
forth, or ever thou hadst formed the
earth & the *world:* even from everlast-
ing to everlasting thou art God, *Psf* 90.

The

The eternal God is thy refuge, and underneath are the everlasting arms.

Now unto the King eternal, immortal, invisible, the only wife God, be honour & glory, for ever & ever. Amen.

And Abraham planted a grove in Beerſheba, & called there on the Name of the LORD, the everlaſting God.

For thus ſaith the high & lofty One that inhabiteth eternity, whoſe Name is holy, I dwell in the high and holy place, with him alſo that is of a contrite and humble ſpirit, to revive the heart of the contrite ones, *Iſa.* 57. 17.

II. *Of GOD's Omnipotency.*

ANd when Abram was ninety years old & nine, the Lord appeared to Abram, & ſaid unto him, I am the Almighty God ; walk before me, and be thou perfect, *Gen.* 17. 1.

I am Alpha and Omega, the Beginning and the Ending, ſaith the Lord, which is, & which was, & which is to come, the Almighty, *Rev.* 1. 8.

And

And I heard as it were the voice of a great multitude, and as the voice of many waters, & as the voice of mighty thundrings, saying, Alleluia : for the Lord God Omnipotent reigneth, *Rev.*

And I appeared unto *Abraham*, unto *Isaac*, & unto *Jacob*, by the Name of GOD Almighty, but by my Name *Jehovah*, was I not known to them. *Exod.6*

His eyes shall see his destruction, and he shall drink of the wrath of the Almighty, *Job* 21. 20.

Ah Lord God, behold thou hast made the Heaven & the Earth, by thy great Power and stretched out Arm, & there is nothing too hard for thee. Great in Counsel & mighty in Work.

Now unto Him that is able to do exceeding abundantly above all that we ask or think, according to the Power that worketh in us, Unto Him be Glory in the Church by Christ Jesus, throughout all Ages, World without end. Amen, *Eph.* 3. 21. *Jer.* 32. 17, 19:

III.

III. *Of GOD's Omnipresence.*

BUt will *God* indeed dwell on earth? Behold the Heaven, & Heaven of Heavens can't contain thee, how much less this house that I have built? 1 *K.* 8

Can any hide himself in secret Places that I shall not see him, saith the Lord.

Whither shall I go from thy Spirit? Or whither shall I flee from thy Presence? If I ascend up into Heaven, thou art there; if I make my bed in Hell, behold thou art there. If I take the wings of the Morning, and dwell in the utmost parts of the Sea, even there shall thy Hand lead me, and thy Right Hand shall hold me. If I say surely the Darkness shall cover me, even the Night shall be light about me. Yea, the Darkness hideth not from thee, but the Night shineth as the Day; the Darkness and the Light are both alike unto thee, *Psal* 139. 7, — 12.

And she called the Name of the Lord that spake unto her, Thou God seest feeſt me; for ſhe ſaid, have I alſo here looked after him that ſeeth me, *Gen.* 16

Thy Father which ſeeth in ſecret ſhall reward thee openly, *Mat.* 6. 4.

Which is his Body, the fulneſs of him that filleth all in all, *Eph.* 1. 23.

IV. *Of GOD's Omniſcience.*

And thou, *Solomon* my Son, know thou the God of thy Father, and ſerve Him with a perfect heart, & with a willing mind : for the Lord Searcheth all hearts and underſtandeth all the Imaginations of the thoughts : if thou ſeek him, he will be found of thee; but if thou forſake him, he will caſt thee off for ever. 1 *Chron.* 28. 9.

Then hear thou in Heaven thy dwelling-place, and forgive; and do, & give to every man according to his ways, whoſe heart thou knoweſt; for thou, even thou only knoweſt the hearts of all the Children of men, 1 *Kin.* 8. 39.

Neither is there any Creature that is not manifeſt in his ſight : but all things

F are

are naked & open to the Eyes of Him
with whom we have to do, *Heb.* 4. 13.

Thou knoweſt my down-ſitting, &
mine upriſing, thou underſtandeſt my
thought afar off.   Thou compaſſeſt
my path, & my lying down, & art ac-
quainted with all my ways. For there
is not a word in my tongue, but lo, O
Lord, thou knoweſt it altogether.

Known unto God are all His
Works from the beginning of the
World, *Acts* 15. 18.

V. *Of the Wiſdom of* GOD:

GReat is our Lord, and of great
power, his underſtanding is
Infinite, *Pſal.* 147. 5.

O the Depth of the Riches, both of
the Wiſdom and Knowlege of God!
How unſearchable are His Judg-
ments, and His Ways paſt finding
out ! *Rom.* 11. 33.

To God only Wiſe, be Glory
through Jeſus Chriſt for Ever. Amen.
Rom. 16. 27.   VI.

VI. *Of the Holiness of* GOD.

ANd one cried unto another, and said, Holy, Holy, Holy, is the Lord of Hosts, the whole Earth is full of His Glory, *Isa.* 6. 3.

And the four Beasts had each of them six wings about him, and they were full of eyes within ; and they rest not Day and Night saying, Holy, Holy, Holy, Lord God Almighty, which was, and is, and is to come, *Rev.* 4. 8.

Because it is written, Be ye holy, for I am Holy, 1 *Pet.* 1. 16:

But thou art Holy, O thou that inhabitest the praises of Israel, *Pf.* 22. 3.

Who shall not Fear thee, O Lord, and Glorify thy Name? For thou art Holy, *Rev.* 15 4.

VII. *Of the Justice of* GOD.

HE is a Rock, His work is perfect : for all His Ways are Judgment : a God of Truth, and without Iniquity, Just and Right is He, *Deut.* 32. 4.

F 2   **Shall**

Shall not the Judge of all the Earth do Right ? *Gen.* 18. 25.

But let him that Glorieth, Glory in this, that he understandeth & knoweth Me that I am the Lord, which exercise Loving kindness, Judgment, & Righteousness in the Earth : for in these things I Deiight saith the Lord, *Jer.* 9.

— And that by no means will clear the guilty ; visiting the Iniquity of the Fathers upon the Children & upon the Childrens Children, unto the third & to the fourth Generation, *Exod.* 34. 7.

He shall Judge the World in Righteousness, he shall minister Judgment to the People in uprightness. The Lord is known by the judgment he executeth. the Wicked is Snared in the work of his own hands, Higgaion. Selah. The wicked shall be turned into Hell & all the Nations that forget God, *Ps.* 9. 8, 16

God shall wound the head of his enemies, and the hairy scalp of such a one as goeth on still in his trespasses, *Ps* 68 VII.

VIII *Of the Truth & Faithfulness of God*

A God of Truth, & without Iniqui-
ty, just & right is he, *Deut.* 32. 4.

His Truth endureth to all Gene-
rations, *Psal.* 100. 5.

Which made Heaven & Earth, the
Sea, & all that therein is: Which keep-
eth Truth for ever. *Psal.* 146. 6.

Now I Nebuchadnezzar Praise &
Extol & Honour the King of Hea-
ven, all whose Works are truth & his
ways judgment, & those that walk in
pride he is able to abase, *Dan.* 4. 17.

All thy Commandments are Truth.

Thou wilt perform the truth to Ja-
cob, & the Mercy to Abraham, which
thou haft sworn unto our Fathers
from the days of old, *Micah* 7. 20.

And hath raised up an horn of Sal-
vation for us, in the House of his Ser-
vant David ; As he spake by the
mouth of his holy Prophets, that have
been since the World began, That we
should be saved from our enemies, &

F 3　　　from

from the Hand of all that hate us. To perform the mercy promised to our Fathers, and to remember his Holy Covenant : The oath which he sware to our Father Abraham, *Luk.* 1. 69, 70

Thy Faithfulness reacheth unto the Clouds, *Psal.* 36. 5.

I will make known thy Faithfulness to all Generations---Thy Faithfulness also in the Congregations of the Saints. But my Faithfulness and my Mercy shall be with him, *Pf.* 89. 1, 2, 5, 24.

Thy Faithfulness is unto all Generations, *Psal.* 119. 90:

IX. *Of the Mercy of GOD.*

ANd the LORD passed by before him, & proclaimed, The LORD, the LORD GOD, Merciful & gracious, long-suffering, & abundant in Goodness and Truth, Keeping Mercy for thousands, forgiving Iniquity, & Transgression, and Sin, *Exod.* 34. 6, 7.

O give Thanks unto the Lord, for he is *good*, for his *Mercy* endureth forever.

GOD

GOD *the Creator of the World.*

THou, even thou art LORD alone, thou haſt made Heaven, the Heaven of Heaven's with all their hoſt, the earth & all things that are therein, the Seas & all that is therein, *Neh.* 9. 6.

And he is before all things, and by him all things conſiſt, *Col.* 1. 16. 17.

For every houſe is builded by ſome man, but he that built all things, is *God.*

GOD *the Governer of the world, in His Works of Providence.*

THE Lord Reigneth, let the earth rejoice, let the multitude of iſles be glad, *Pſal.* 97. 1.

The King's heart is in the hand of the LORD, as the Rivers of water, he turneth it whitherſoever he will, *P.* 21

The lot is caſt into the lap : but the whole diſpoſing thereof is of the Lord, *Prov.* 16. 33.

Upholding all things by the word of his power, *Heb.* 1. 3.

His Kingdom ruleth over all, *Pſ.* 103

Who

Who worketh all things after the counsel of his own will, *Eph.* 1. 11.

The State of Man before the Fall.

SO God Created man in His own Image, in the Image of God created he him, Male & Female created he them. And God bleſſed them, & God ſaid unto them, be fruitful and multiply, and repleniſh the earth, & ſubdue it ; and have dominion over the fiſh of the ſea, over the fowl of the air, and over every living thing that moveth upon the earth, *Gen.* 1. 27, 28.

And have put on the new Man, which is renewed in knowlege, after the Image of him that created him.

And that ye put on the new Man, which after God is Created in Righteouſneſs, & true Holineſs, *Eph.* 4. 24.

Lo, this only have I found, that *God* made man upright.

Of the Fall of Man.

— BUt they have ſought out many Inventions, *Eccl.* 7. 29.

And

And when the woman saw that the tree was good for food, and that it was pleasant to the eyes, & a tree to be desired to make one wise: she took of the fruit thereof, & did eat. *Gen.* 3.6

Wherefore as by one man Sin entred into the world, and death by sin, and so death hath passed upon all men, for that all have sinned, *Rom.* 5.

For since by man came Death, by Man came also the resurrection of the dead; For as in Adam all die, even so in Christ shall all be made alive, 1 *Cor.*

O Israel, thou hast destroyed thyself, but in Me is thine help. *Hos.* 13.9.

Thy first Father hath sinned, *Is.* 43

The way of Fallen Man's Recovery by Christ.

I Will put Enmity between thee & the Woman, & between thy Seed & her Seed; it shall bruise thy head, and thou shalt bruise his heel, *Gen.* 3.

And she shall bring forth a Son & thou shalt call his Name Jesus; for he shall

ſhall ſave his people from their Sins

For unto you is born this Day, in the city of David, a Saviour, which is Chriſt the Lord, *Luk.* 2. 11.

For the Son of Man is come to ſeek and to ſave that which was Loſt.

This is a faithful ſaying and worthy of all acceptation, that Chriſt Jeſus came into the world to ſave Sinners, of whom I am chief, 1 *Tim.* 1. 15.

Neither is there Salvation in any other : for there is none other name under Heaven given among men whereby we muſt be ſaved, *Act.* 4. 12.

Of Death.

FOr the wages of Sin is Death : but the gift of God is Eternal life, thro' Jeſus Chriſt our Lord, *Rom* 6. 23

--- For in the Day that thou eateſt thereof, thou ſhall ſurely Die, *Gen.* 2. 17 The end of thoſe things is death. *Rom.* 6

Of the Reſurrection & laſt Judgment.

MArvel not at this : for the hour is coming, in the which all that

that are in their Graves ſhall hear His Voice, And ſhall come forth, they that have done good unto the Reſurrection of life ; and they that have done evil, unto the Reſurrection of Damnation, *Joh.* 5. 28, 29.

For we muſt all appear before the Judgment-ſeat of Chriſt, that every one may receive the things done in his body, according to that he hath done, whether it be good or bad, 2 *Cor.* 5. 10

Of Heaven.

FOr we know, that if our earthly houſe of this tabernacle were diſſolved, we have a building of God, an houſe not made with hands, eternal in the Heavens, 2 *Cor.* 5. 1.

— To day thou ſhalt be with me in Paradiſe, *Luk.* 23. 43.

—- Eye hath not ſeen, nor ear heard, neither have entered into the heart of man, the things which God hath prepared for them that love Him, 1 *Cor.* 2. 9.

Of

Of Hell.

——THE Rich man died and was buried. And in Hell he lift up his eyes, being in Torments, & feeth *Abraham* afar off, and *Lazarus* in his bofom. And he cried and faid, Father *Abraham*, have mercy on me, and fend *Lazarus*, that he may dip the tip of his finger in water, and cool my tongue; for I am Tormented in this Flame, *Luk.* 16. 22, 23, 24.

Where their Worm dieth not, and the Fire is not quenched, *Mark* 9. 44.

And thefe fhall go away into Everlafting Punifhment, *Mat.* 25. 46.

The Bleffings of the Righteous in the World to Come.

WIth everlafting Joy, *Ifa.* 61. 7
With everlafting Life, *Job.* 3. 16
With everlafting Glory, 2 *Cor.* 4. 17.
With everlafting Honour, *Rom.* 2. 7.
With everlafting Liberty, 2 *Cor.* 3. 17
With everlafting Light, *Pfal.* 97. 11.
With everlafting Dominion, *Pf* 49. 14

The

The Curses of the Wicked.

With everlasting Shame, *Dan.* 12.2
With everlasting Death, *Ibid.*
With everlasting Contempt, *Job.* 12.
With everlasting Slavery, *Job.* 15.20,
With everlasting Bondage, *Isa.* 3.11.
With everlasting Darkness, *Mat.* 8.12
With everlasting Destruction, 2 *Thes.* 1

CHAP. VII.

Containing Eleven short Exhortations.

1 Let thy Thoughts be Divine, Awful and Godly.

2 Let thy Talk be Little, Honest and True.

3 Let thy Works be Profitable, Holy and Charitable.

4 Let thy Manners be Grave, Courteous and Chearful.

5 Let thy Diet be Temperate, Convenient and Frugal.

6 Let thy Apparel be Sober, Neat and Comely,

G

7 Let

7 Let thy Will be Compliant, Obedient and Ready.

8 Let thy Sleep be Moderate, Quiet, and Seasonable.

9 Let thy Prayers be Devout, Often and Fervent.

10 Let thy Recreation be Lawful, Brief and Seldom.

11 Let thy Meditations be of Death, Judgment and Eternity.

CHAP. VIII.

Containing §. I. *Good Thoughts for Children.*

A verse may find him whom a sermon flies
And turn Delight into a Sacrifice.

I Was Baptiz'd unto the LORD,
　Who FATHER, SON and SPIRIT is.
I must Fear GOD, & Mind His Word,
And Look to CHRIST for Happiness

　The GOD of Heaven did make me,
That I to Him should Subject be.
The Son of GOD is Man Become,
That he to God might *bring man home.*

If

If I Believe in JESUS CHRIST,
Then I shall be for ever Blest ;
But if I Slight that Saviour Kind,
My Misery will Never End.

THe Living GOD, I must Adore,
   As he requires, *him come Before,*
His Holy Name, Take not in Vain,
His Holy Day, Never Prophane,
To all Superiors, Honour Give,
Take care, *that nei° bours well may live,*
Keep clear from all Unchastity,
Refrain from all Dishonesty,
That all my speech be Truth, *take heed*
All shews of Discontentment Dread.

Beg pardning Grace for all Sins past,
Trust Christ, my Soul to Save, at Last.

Thus the Commandments may be Versifi'd
1 HAve thou no other Gods but Me.
   2 Unto no Image bow thy Knee.
3 Take not the Name of God in Vain.
4 Do not the Sabbath-day Profane.
5 Honour thy Father, Mother too.
6 Take heed that thou no Murder do:

      G 2   6 From

7 From Whoredom *keep thy body clean.*
8 Steal not, altho' thy State be mean.
9 Bear not false Witness, *shun that blot.*
10 What is thy Nei'bours Covet not.

These are the Laws which God did give:
Keep them by Faith in Christ, & Live.

---

§. II. *A compendious Body of Divinity.*

THE *Scriptures* of divine Authority
   A perfect *rule* for all men to walk by
From them we learn the living God,
         to know.
And what the duty is we to him owe.
Three sacred Persons *in the God-head be*
Of one Power, Substance & Eternitie:
The Father, & Christ Jesus, his own Son
The Holy Ghost; and all these
         Three are ONE.
God is a most Pure Spirit, Infinite,
In Truth abundant, of great Power
         and Might.

                              Most

Moſt Holy, Wiſe, Juſt, Good,
    Long-Suffering,
Of *whom*, thro' *whom*, to *whom* is
    every thing.
He made the World, and all that
    is therein :
Man was made Upright, but ſoon fell
    by Sin.
We all do from *polluted Parents* ſpring
And in our *fleſh* there dwelleth no
    good thing.
None Righteous are, *but all of every
    ſort,*
Have Sinn'd, and of God's Glory
    are come ſhort.
But God ſo Loved us that he did give,
His only Son that we thro' Him
    might live.
The Son of God became the *Son of man,*
That we might be the *Sons of God again*
He's God and Man ; the only
    Mediator.
Between the Sons of Men and their
    Creator.

       He

He gave Himſelf for our eternal good
& *waſht away our ſins by his own blood.*
What *love* was this ? twas *love* be-
        yond degree,
The Offended dies to ſet the Offen-
        ders free.
It's God that juſtifies ; who ſhall
        condemn ?
It's *Chriſt* that *dy'd,* or rather *roſe again*
Who alſo ſits at God's right Hand
        on High ;
And Interceeds for Us continually.
We by one Spirit thorow Him alone,
May have acceſs unto the Holy One.
If we believe on him that came to *ſave*
We're ſure at laſt eternal Life to have.
There's nothing that avails with God
        above,
But Faith in Jeſus Chriſt; which
        works by Love.
Hereby we know that we do love
        the Lord,
When we do keep the Precepts of
        his Word.

                  The

The Lord hath shew'd what he re-
quires as good,
Deal justly and walk humbly with
your God.
Serve *him* with *fear*, love *him* with
all your might ;
Speak ill of none, and give to all
their right.
And when you have done all you
can, confess
The imperfection of your Righte-
ousness.
Ascribe the Praise of all the Good
you do,
To Him that works the Will and
Deed in you.
Keep Conscience pure and void of
all offence :
Prepare for death with *speed & diligence*
Bless are the dead that in the Lord do dy
Their works do follow them assuredly
The day is coming when the dead
shall hear,
The voice of Christ, and forthwith
shall appear.   All

All they to Life whose works are
          good and right :
All they to death who do in Sin delight
As every man hath in the Body done,
So shall his *Sentence* at the *last day* run.
The wicked shall be turned into hell,
The Righteous   shall   with *Christ*
          for ever dwell.

---

§ III. *An Alphabet of useful Copies.*

AT Table guard thy Tongue, a
          civil Guest,
Will *no more talk all*, than eat all
          the *feast*.

BE well Advis'd and wary Counsel
          take,
Er'e thou dost any Action undertake

COmmand thyself in chief, he life's
          war knows
Whom all his Passions follow, as
          he goes.

DAre to be true, *nothing* can
          need a Lie :
A fault that needs it most grows
     two thereby.   En-

ENdeavour so to Live, & so to Die,
 As to Enjoy a bleſt Eternity.

FIrſt worſhip God : he that forgets
 to Pray
Bids not himſelf good morrow, nor
 good day.

GO, run, ride, ſwim, uſe every
 honeſt way,
Rather than Poverties command obey

HOw dare you ſin in ſecret ? God
 doth ſee
And will alone thy Judge & Jury be.

IF a Son makes his Fathers heart
 to bleed,
He may a Child have to revenge the
 deed.

KEep thy ſelf humble, Pride has
 ruin'd many,
The proud man's ſeldom well be-
 lov'd of any.

LOve covers multitudes of faults,
 but hate
Old faults diſcovers, and does new
 ones make.

Men.

MEn for this worlds poor riches
are at strife,
Neglecting those of everlasting Life.

NO wonder if the best men some-
times fail,
Since all are mortal, and their natures
frail.

OUr faults, our friends, and our in-
structions, we
Are strangely subject to forget these
three.

PLeasure is fleeting still, and makes
no stay,
It lends a smile or two, & steals away

QUaint wits with words, and posies
windows fill,
Less than least *Mercies*, is my posie still

RAther depend upon your fingers
ends,
Than fix your expectations on your
friends.

SWear not, an Oath is like a dange-
rous dart.
Which shot rebounds to hit the
shooters heart. The

THe Drunkard forfeits man, and
doth divest
All worldly right, save what he hath
by beast.

USe Patience what e're haps,
tho' bad it be,
Take it for good, and 'twill be so
to thee.

WHose, where, and what thou
art, Consider well :
And think on *Death, Judgment,
Heaven,* and *Hell.*

X *Erxes* with tears surveys his
mighty *Host,*
Thinking how soon they'd all be
dead and lost.

YOuth is the flower of age, the
May of time,
Then catch occasion in its proper
clime.

ZEal, thou shalt be my chariot
whilst I ride,
Elijah-like, with sacred writ my
Guide.

§ IV.

§. IV. Cyprian's *Twelve Absurdities.*

ONE void of good Works among the Wise inroll'd

2 A man without *religion when he's old*

3 A man in youth without obedience.

4 A wealthy man who do's not alms recompense.

5 A woman *shameless* with a brazen *face*

6 A guide that Vice, not Vertue doth imbrace.

7 A Christian who Contention doth maintain.

8 One in whom Poverty and Pride doth reign.

9 A King or Governor who is unjust.

10 A Bishop who neglects his Charge and Trust.

11 A *people* who will not be *disciplin'd*

12 And Subjects whom no Laws suffice to bind.

Cyprian's *Twelve Absurdities* are these,
Take them as Warnings if you please.

F   I   N   I   S,

The Prodigal Daughter

Bibliographical Note:

This facsimile has been made
from a copy in the
Free Library of Philadelphia.
(ROS70)

This title has been
reduced thirty percent.

THE
PRODIGAL DAUGHTER;

Or a strange and wonderful relation, shewing, how a
Gentleman of a vast Estate in BRISTOL, had a proud
and disobedient Daughter, who because her parents
would not support her in all her extravagance, bargained
with the Devil to poison them. How an Angel inform-
ed her parents of her design. How she lay in a trance
four days ; and when she was put in the grave, she
came to life again, &c. &c.

BOSTON, printed and sold at I. THOMAS's Printing-Of-
fice near the MILL BRIDGE.

(1771)

THE

PRODIGAL DAUGHTER:

OR, THE

Difobedient Lady reclaimed, &c.

LET every wicked gracelefs child attend,
   And liften to thefe lines that here are pen'd,
GOD grant it may to all a warning be,
To love their friends and fhun bad company.

No further off than Briftol now of late,
A gentleman liv'd of a vaft eftate,
And he had but one only daughter fair :
Whom he moft tenderly did love fo dear.

They kept her cloath'd in coftly rich array,
And as the child grew up, for truth they fay,
Her heart with pride was lifted up fo high,
She fix'd her whole delight in vanity.

Each

Each sinful course to her did pleasant seem,
And of the holy scriptures made a game :
At length her parents did begin to see,
Their tender kindness would her ruin be.

Her mother thus to her began to speak,
My child this course you run my heart will break,
The tender love which we to you have shown,
I fear, will cause our tender hearts to groan.

Come, come, my child, this course in time refrain,
And serve the LORD now in your youthful prime,
For if in this your wicked course you run,
Your soul and body both will be undone.

Laughing and scoffing, at her mother, she
Said, pray now, trouble not yourself with me,
Why do you talk to me of heav'ns joy,
My youthful pleasures all for to destroy.

I am not certain what I shall possess,
After I have resign'd my vital breath ;
I nothing for another world do care,
Therefore I'll take my pleasure while I'm here.

The mother said, my child, how do you know,
How soon your pride into the dust will go?
For young as well as old to death bow down,
And you must die, GOD only know's how soon.

She from her mother in a passion went,
Filling her aged heart with discontent:
She rung her hands, and to her husband said,
She's ruin'd soul and body I'm affraid.

Her father said, her pride I will pull down,
Money to spend of me she shall have none,
I'll make her humble before I have done,
Or else forever I will her disown.

All night she from her father's house did stray,
Next morning she came home by break of day,
Her father he did ask her where she'd been?
She straightway answer'd, what was that to him.

He said, your haughty pride I will pull down,
Money to spend no more I'll give you none,
She said, if you deny me what I crave,
I'll sell my soul but money I will have.

Her father stript her of her rich array,
And then he cloath'd her in a russet gray,
And to her chamber did her confine,
With bread and water fed her for some time.

Altho' their hearts for her did ake full sore,
This course they took her soul for to restore,
But all in vain she wanted Heaven's grace
And sin within her heart had taken place,

One night as in her room she musing were,
The Devil in her room did then appear,
And seemingly he took her by the hand,
In shape and person like a gentleman.

He said fair creature, why do you lament ?
Why is your heart thus fill'd with discontent ?
She said, my parents cruel are to me,
And keep me here to starve in misery.

    The devil said, if you'll be rul'd by me,
Reveng'd on them you certainly shall be,
Seem to be humble, tell them you'll repent,
And soon you'll find their hearts for to relent.

And when your father he doth use you kind,
An opportunity you soon will find,
Poison your father and your mother too,
There's none will know who 'twas the fact did do.

This wicked wretch quite void of grace and shame,
She seem'd to be well pleas'd at the same ;
Said I'm resolv'd your council for to take,
And be reveng'd for what they've done of late,

Where do you live, pray tell me where to come,
That I may tell you when the jobb is done ?
He said, my name is Satan, and I dwell
In the dark regions of the burning hell.

At first she seem'd to be somewhat surpriz'd
But want of grace so blinded had her eyes,
She said, well sir, if you the Devil be,
I'll take the counsel which you gave to me.

But mind what wonders GOD doth every hour,
His mercies are above the Devil's pow'r,
He will his servants keep both night and day
From the devouring subtle serpent's prey.

Next day when she her father's face did see,
She instantly did fall upon her knee,
Saying, father now my wicked heart relents,
And for my sins I heartily repent.

Her father then with tears did her embrace,
Saying I'm blest for this small spark of grace,
That Heaven hath my child bestow'd on thee,
No more I'll use you with such cruelty.

Unto her mother then straitway he goes,
And told to her the blest and happy news.
Her mother was rejoic'd then for her part,
Not knowing the mischief that was in her heart,

But the Almighty her defigns did know,
And 'twas his bleffed will it fhould be fo,
That other gracelefs children they might fee,
All things are done by Heav'ns great decree.

The poifon ftrong fhe privately had bought,
And only then the fatal time fhe fought,
To work the fall of thefe her parents dear,
Who'd brought her up with tender love and care.

One night her parents fleeping were in bed,
Nothing but troubled dreams run in their heads;
At length an Angel did to them appear,
Saying awake and unto me give ear.

A messenger I'm sent by Heaven kind,
To let you know your deaths are both design'd
Your graceless child whom you do love so dear,
She for your precious lives hath laid a snare.

To poison you the Devil tempts her so,
She hath no power from the snare to go,
But GOD such care doth of his servants take,
Those that believe on him he'll not forsake.

You must not use her cruel nor severe,
For tho' these things to you I do declare,
It is to shew you what the LORD can do,
He soon can turn her heart, you'll find it so.

Pray to the LORD his grace for to send down,
And like the prodigal she will return,
The fatted calf with joy you'll kill that day,
The Angels shall rejoice in Heaven high.

Because a wretched sinner doth repent,
Who in vice and sin her time hath all misspent.
This pious couple then awoke, we hear,
And soon the Angel he did disappear.

They to each other did the vision tell,
And from this time we'll mark her actions well,
And if this vision unto pass must come,
We'll praise the LORD for such great favours done.

Next morning she rose early, as we hear,
And for her parents breakfast did prepare,
And in the same she put the poison strong,
And brought it unto them when she had done.

Her father took the victuals which she brought.
And down the same unto the dog he set,
Who ate the food and instantly did die,
The case was plain she could not it deny.

B

They call'd her there the fight for to behold,
Which when she saw, her spirits soon ran cold,
She cry'd the Devil hath me now deceiv'd,
I've mist my aim for which I'm sorely griev'd.

Her mother cry'd, hard is the fate of me,
I've been a tender mother unto thee,
And can you seek to take my life away,
O graceless child ! What will become of thee ?

With bitter pains my child, I did you bear,
I taught you how the LORD of life to fear,
Whole days and nights I did in sorrow spend,
To bring you up now to my discontent.

Quite void of grace you in your sins do run,
You slight my counsel after all I've done,
Instead of obedience which you ought to pay,
Your parents lives you're seeking to betray.

When thus she heard her tender mother speak,
She in a swoon did drop down at her feet,
And all the arts that e're they could contrive,
They could not bring her spirits to revive.

Four days they kept her, when they did prepare
To lay her body in the dust we hear,
At her funeral a sermon then was preach'd,
All other wicked children for to teach :

How they should fear their tender parents kind,
Their words observe, their counsel for to mind,
And then their days will long be in this land,
All things shall prosper which they take in hand.

So close the Reverend divine did lay
This charge, that many wept that there did stay
To hear the sermon, and her parents dear
Were over-whelm'd with sorrow, grief and care.

The sermon being over and quite done,
To lay her body in the dust they came,
But suddenly they bitter groans did hear,
Which much surpriz'd all that then were there.

At length they did observe the dismal sound,
Came from the body just laid in the ground,
The coffin then they did draw up again,
And in a fright they opened the same,

When soon they found that she was yet alive,
Her mother seeing that she did survive,
Did praise the LORD, in hopes she would have time,
And would repent of all her heinous crimes.

She in her coffin then was carried home,
And when unto her father's house she came,
She in her coffin sat and did admire
Her winding sheet, and then she did desire,

The worthy minister for to sit down,
And she would tell him wonders which was shown
Unto her since her soul had took it's flight,
She had seen the regions of eternal night.

She said, when first my soul did hence depart,
For to relate the story grieves my heart,
I handed was to lonesome wild deserts,
And briery woods which dismal were and dark.

The briars tore my flesh, the gore did run,
I cry'd for mercy, but I could find none,
I at length a little glimpse of light did spy,
And heard a voice which unto me did cry :

Now sinful soul observe and you shall see,
How precious does that light appear to thee !
But in dark regions of eternal night,
You never must expect for to see light.

Now hasten to that light which does appear,
And there your sentence you will quickly hear,
I hearing this did hasten then along,
At length unto a spacious gate I come.

I knock'd aloud, but on one answer made,
At length one did to me appear and said,
What want you here ? I answer'd to come in,
He ask'd my name, then shut the gate again.

He stay'd a while, then to the door did come,
He said, begone, for you there is no room,
For we have no such graceless wretches here,
That disobey their tender parents dear.

I sorely wept, and to the man thus said,
Am I the first that parents disobey'd ?
If I be cast to Hell who thus do sin,
Few at this gate I fear will enter in.

He said, but you have been a sinner wild,
In things besides a disobedient child,
Swearing and whoring, sabbath breaking too,
Therefore begone; for here's no rest for you.

I said, sir hear me, and remember pray,
How holy David he did run astray,
The man whose heart once with the LORD did join,
Adultery and murder was his crime.

He said like David you did not return,
For he in ashes for his sins did mourn,
And GOD is merciful you well do know,
Free to forgive all those that humble so,

I still my case with him pursu'd to plead,
And told him Sir in scripture I do read,
How Mary Magdalen, who here doth rest,
At once by many devils was possest.

Go, silly woman, he did answer then,
Had you so much lamented for your sin,
And mercy at your Saviour's feet implor'd,
For all your sins, he had your soul restor'd.

I said, in person she her Saviour saw,
He said, you may behold him ev'ry day,
He ne'er leaves those who in his mercy trust,
He's always with the pious, good and just.

In holy scripture he doth there appear,
Read the apostles and you'll find him there,
You must believe, if that you sav'd will be,
That CHRIST, for sinners dy'd upon a tree.

Then save me LORD I to him did reply,
For I believe that CHRIST did for me die;
LORD, let my soul return from whence it came,
And I will honour thy most holy name.

A voice I heard which said to me return,
But first behold the wretched place of doom,
Where the reward of sin is justly paid,
I turn'd about, but sadly was dismay'd.

I saw the burning lake of misery.
I saw the man there that first tempted me
My loving tender parents for to stay,
And he both fierce and grim did look at me.

He told me, he at last was sure of me,
I said my Saviour's blood has set me free:
Then in a hideous manner he did roar,
When GOD my senses did to me restore.

When thus the story she to them had told,
She said put me to bed for I am cold,
And call to me my tender parents dear,
Whom I will love and honour while I'm here.

To take the sacrament she did require,
They gave it her then, as she did desire,
And now she is a christian just and true,
No more her wicked vices does pursue.

I hope this will a good example be,
Children your parents honour and obey,
And then the LORD will bless you here on earth,
And give you a crown of glory after death.

T H E

Substance of a SERMON,

Preached on the occasion.

Luke XV. and the firſt part of the 24th verſe.
" *For this my ſon was dead, and is alive, he was loſt and*
" *is found.*"

IN the preaching this ſermon, the Reverend Mr. WIL-
LIAMS was pleaſed on this occaſion to obſerve,

Firſt, How, when people fall into ſin, they are dead to
grace, and how miſerable a thing it is to be in a ſtate of
damnation, which all thoſe who are in diſobedience to
their parents lawful commands aſſuredly are.

Secondly, What it is to be " dead, and alive again," by
returning from ſin, as the prodigal ſon did ; in which
part he very largely diſcourſed on the rejoicings made
in Heaven, for the ſake of a ſinner's repentance.

Thirdly and laſtly, He explained what was meant by
thoſe words, " he was loſt and is found," viz. That by
a man's falling into ſin, he is loſt to GOD : But by re-
turning to grace he ſhall find mercy at the throne there-
of and cloſes the whole with the wonderful mercies of
GOD, in calling this young lady to repentance.

F I N I S.

CHILDREN'
LITERATUR
...